GROWING SANE

Psychological Disturbances
Accompanying the
Growth of Consciousness

James Stallone, Ph.D.
Sy Migdal, Ph.D.

Upshur Press
Dallas, PA

GROWING SANE

PSYCHOLOGICAL DISTURBANCES
ACCOMPANYING THE
GROWTH OF CONSCIOUSNESS
By
James Stallone, Ph.D.
Sy Migdal, Ph.D.

Library of Congress Cataloging-in-Publication Data

Stallone, James, 1937-
    Growing sane : psychological disturbances accompanying the
growth of consciousness / James Stallone, Sy Migdal.
        p.   cm.
    Includes index.
    ISBN 0-912975-06-7 (soft) $11.95
    1. Mental illness–Popular works.   2. Psychotherapy–Popular
works. 3. Maturation (Psychology) 4. Consciousness.
I. Migdal, Sy. 1937- . II. Title.
RC454.4.S72   1991
616.89–dc20
                                                91-75033
                                                    CIP

Notice–The publisher and authors caution you not to attempt
diagnosis or embark upon self-treatment of serious illness
without competent professional assistance. We encourage
anyone who is experiencing distress beyond the scope of this
book to seek competent professional advice. Also, if you are
under professional care or taking medication, we suggest
discussing any changes in life style with your doctor.

Published by Upshur Press, P. O. Box 609,
Dallas, Pennsylvania 18612-0609

Design Assistance - Anthony Stallone
Typesetting - Ola Mae Schoonover

More than fifteen years have passed since we formulated the concepts presented in **Growing Sane** as the basis for helping people in counseling, therapy, and educational settings. The test of time and experience has refined our understanding of the psychological disturbances accompanying the growth of consciousness and verified the treatments prescribed. During this decade, noticeable and significant developments of consciousness have taken place in the lives of many individuals and collectively for the entire globe. From our own experience and observation, we have seen a growing interest and research in the expansion of consciousness, as well as increasing reports of positive experiences in individuals throughout the world. As we had anticipated, along with these experiences have come the attendant disturbances that accompany the growth of consciousness.

Because more and more people are reporting deeper and broader experiences of that one reality we call consciousness or awareness, the need is even greater for recognition, understanding, natural measures, and techniques to stabilize, integrate, and encourage the smooth continuation of this process. Globally, at this moment, we are seeing the dramatic effects of more people "growing sane" through continued expansion of science and technology, responsible environmental action, the social, political, and economic unity of nations, and the prospects for world peace. Even with the inevitable setbacks, the overall effect has still been encouraging.

One of the new concepts that we have added to our basic theory is our recognition of the necessity for those "on the path to Enlightenment" to become adults in the fullest sense of the word. To become adult means to become independent through successfully accomplishing what psychologists call "separation-individuation" on the physical, intellectual, social, moral, vocational/financial levels, and most important, the ego/emotional level. For many individuals, this may mean having to "back up" and "grow up" in areas or stages of life that were missed, glossed over, or put aside as unworthy of attention.

Far too many "seekers" are stuck at the child-adolescent stage, never having established adulthood nor experienced being "on their own." They mistakenly believe they can substitute the experience of "growing sane" for the prerequisite of "growing up;" and in making this mistake, they accomplish neither goal. Recognition of this prerequisite of growing up is humbling, but it's also a necessary step for those in search of "higher" truth.

Also, we have become increasingly and sharply aware of the necessity to insist that some individuals who are undergoing particularly disturbing accelerated growth avail themselves of the resources the "establishment" has to offer. These might include conventional services from medical, psychological, social, or economic resources.

Probably not one growth or spiritual group existing has not had its share of casualties regarding serious physical illness, psychosis, suicide proneness, or economic, social and familial deterioration. But these symptoms must be dealt with effectively. Frequently, "old age" rather than "new age" is the preferred and more effective treatment of choice. This does not mean that "new age" or holistic techniques don't work, because they do. However, when for some reason they don't address immediate concerns, more conventional approaches may be necessary. This is especially true in emergency or crisis situations.

Knowing when to seek outside help is the ethical responsibility of any individual, professional, growth group, or spiritual movement. In Appendix A we further address this matter of when to seek outside help for yourself or someone else.

Finally, we are certain that future editions of this book will address the masses of those "growing sane" rather than the exceptions we first identified and set out to serve when we first formulated our ideas. We look forward to it! We dedicate this book to that ever-increasing segment of society who are experiencing the growth of consciousness and want to facilitate the process.

James Stallone, Ph.D.
Sy Migdal, Ph.D.
1991

One
Mental Wellness

Although we are far from living in an ideal society and world, there are still many signs today which tell us that we are living in a very special age. This is an age which will be remembered not just for the progress it has made in science and technology, and for its higher standards with regard to the environment, justice and world peace, but also for the advances that have been made in the growth of human consciousness. Never before, at least in the recent history of Western Civilization, have so many people from so many walks of life decided to pursue this goal. Many names have been given to this goal: "full potential," "enlightenment," "personal freedom," "liberation," "self-realization," or simply "growth." But no matter what we call the goal, the search is essentially the same.

At one time, we associated the goal of enlightenment with monks who left the world and secluded themselves in forests and caves. But today millions of people pursue this goal, and they range from suburban housewives to small-town businessmen, from the skeptic to the devoutly religious individual, from the athlete to the scientist, and from the young to the very old. A seeker after enlightenment could just as well be wearing a striped three-piece business suit as a pair of overalls and work shoes.

Our goal here in this book is not to try to analyze the reasons for this continuing popular interest in the growth of consciousness or the many techniques and programs used to facilitate that growth. We share the belief of many others that what is happening, by whatever means (your own, or someone else's), is not just a passing fad, but a real revolution–a revolution which will bring about a new age for mankind and will result in higher, advanced ways of thinking, living, loving, and being.

We are concerned with what is happening to you as an individual as you try to achieve these personal and planetary goals. Many of the changes that are taking place in your life may be unexpected. We want to explain these changes to you so that you understand them and have practical and effective ways of dealing with them.

But first of all, what do we mean by "unexpected" changes? Since you have decided, by whatever means, to make this journey toward complete growth, you have also obviously decided to accept the changes which will naturally occur on the journey. After all, it is because you are more than willing to accept changes in your life that you have decided to go from a limited concept of yourself to a full flowering of the person you really can be. However, what you may not be so prepared to accept is that the changes on the road to your full potential can often be very confusing and disturbing.

Your goal is a fully developed mind and body. But if you are like most people on the path toward this goal, you are probably not making progress in steady and ever increasing steps of health and happiness. Instead, you are moving in fits and starts, sometimes going forward, sometimes getting stuck in one place, sometimes even seeming to go backward.

If you have ever been in such a situation of frustration and confusion and have sought understanding and professional help, you will likely have found that ordinary psychology is not able to explain the psychological disturbances that accompany the growth of consciousness or to offer much real help in meeting the special needs that you face in these periods of transition. In these cases conventional psychotherapy may be all too ready to step in with theories of mental illness, inappropriate techniques, and labels that do not apply to you; or with drugs that will stop the disturbing symptoms you are feeling, but will also stop the growth which produces these symptoms in the first place.

If this is your situation, your need is not for labels of mental illness or tranquilizing drugs, but rather for real understanding of what the growth of consciousness actually means in your daily life. We need to be able to stabilize the gains we have already made and to move forward with confidence and assurance; and we want to be able to use the gains we have made in our daily lives so that we can become healthier and happier people.

Our purpose in this book is twofold; first we want to give you the understanding you need so when you face confusion and doubt on your path toward full development you will know what is happening to you. Secondly, we want you not just to understand what is happening, but to be able to do something about it. Both purposes are very important. Clear understanding will erase much of your confusion; practical techniques will allow you to go on to make real progress in your growth.

Let's begin, first of all, with a general idea of what we mean by the growth of consciousness. You can best understand this idea if you see it in the light of the whole concept of evolution. Now by evolution we do not mean how the world began. We mean how the world is today, right now, in front of our eyes.

We know from science and from our own observation that the world we live in is always changing and always changing in the specific direction of growth and maturity. A tiny seed grows into a beautiful, complex, towering tree. Living things from tiny microscopic organisms to plants, to birds and mammals, are busy all the time maintaining their lives. But more than just maintaining our lives, all of us are trying to grow to our fullest and most complete level of maturity. As the lyrics of a popular song say, "Those not busy being born, are busy dying."

Now what we need to realize is that growth and evolution are not only physical, they are also psychological. Of course, there is not as much evidence for evolution of the mind as there is for evolution of the physical world. There are lots of reasons for this lack of evidence, but probably the most important reason is that until recently we have been much more interested in discovering how the physical world unfolds than in discovering how the psychological or inner world unfolds.

But even just our knowledge of physical evolution can lead us to conclude that the evolution of consciousness is a reality. The reason for this is that science has established an intimate connection between states of body and states of mind; so nothing happens to the body without happening to the mind. To take a simple example, when we are asleep, the mind is in a certain state of activity, or in this case, inactivity.

At the same time, the body acts accordingly. If you were in one room and scientists were in another room with the right kind of instruments hooked up to your body, they could tell when you were asleep or when you were awake–just by certain changes in your body. Similarly, if you started to dream, they would know this by certain changes in your body's behavior.

Even mental moods have their corresponding state of body. If we are angry, that is not just an unhealthy state of mind, but also an unhealthy state of body. If you have ever felt "butterflies" in your stomach when you were nervous, you know what we mean.

So, because we know with certainty that there is such an intimate connection between mind and body, we see there cannot be physical evolution without psychological evolution. In our own age, we have made incredible strides in the area of material progress. No doubt there are many problems to solve, but our advances in science and technology, the explosion of knowledge, increased standards of living for more and more people, all point to progress. Certainly our age will be looked at by future generations as one of very high achievement.

Now the basis of this material progress lies in our own creativity. Great achievements such as landing on the moon, increased food production, splitting the atom, or the polio vaccine, do not happen by themselves. They are the result of people's actions, and the action is itself based on the inner creative intelligence of the people performing the action. Expanded creative intelligence on the inside leads to greater achievements on the outside.

So just on the basis of recent achievements in the material world, we can conclude that we are living in an age of expanded creative intelligence. But in this age we are beginning to focus on our inner creativity, to understand our own minds. We are doing this through increased understanding of psychology and through a variety of self-improvement and consciousness expanding techniques.

Just as our increased understanding of outer nature is not just theoretical, but has a real practical value, the same is true of our understanding of our inner nature. Any theory of the mind which has real value must have as its goal not just understanding, but using that understanding to make us happier and more creative people. Whether we call it greater creative intelligence, increased awareness, or the growth of consciousness, this has become an area where more and more people are directing more and more energy.

The practical goal of all concepts of psychological growth is the living reality of enlightenment, or simply put, the development of our full potential. With the prospect of tremendous achievement in the outer as well as inner plane, we can truly agree with those seers of our time who have already announced the dawning of the "Age of Enlightenment," "the "New Age," or similar terms.

Now this new age must give birth to a psychology which not only aims to help people with serious mental illness, but also takes into account the full range and splendid development of human consciousness. This is really a pressing need of our time. As more and more of us become actively involved in advancing our own personal development, we experience profound change in our lives. We need simple and workable explanations for these changes.

The most important requirement for such an explanation is that it clearly differentiates those disturbances that accompany the growth of consciousness from serious mental illness that requires complex and extensive treatment. For those of you on the path to higher consciousness, such explanations are vitally important, as they will help you to pass over obstacles and continue making progress toward your ultimate goal.

Probably the first questions we would want to raise in any explanation are these: Is there really a unique characteristic of those psychological disturbances that accompany the growth of consciousness, what we may call in brief a "growth crisis"? What is the real difference between a growth crisis and the disturbances described by traditional psychological labels such as "schizophrenia" or "manic depressive psychosis"?

If you are experiencing symptoms of a growth crisis, it might seem at first glance that these are symptoms of actual deep psychological disturbances. You experience the same sort of anxiety, doubt, confusion, depression, anger and uncomfortable bodily sensations. **However, if what is happening to you is, in fact, a genuine growth crisis, then you are aware of what is happening while the disturbance is taking place.** This self-awareness is by far the most distinctive feature of the growth crisis and to help you recognize, understand, and deal with it is one of the most important tasks of this book.

A person who is experiencing this self-awareness seems as if he or she is on the outside watching or witnessing the disturbances that are taking place. It is as if you are watching a drama in which you yourself are the main actor. This is not to say that the role you are playing is a pleasant one; there may be anxiety, angry moods or depressions that obviously you would rather not be experiencing.

Or, you may be playing a very confusing role. You wonder, "What is the meaning of all this? Why am I doing or saying or feeling these things?" But the important point is that through all of these disturbances there is a part of you that knows you are just **playing** the role–you are not the role. Now it may be that you are unable to stop playing the role; still your basic awareness or consciousness is not completely overcome or overshadowed by the moods and feelings of the role. Always, there is the feeling of watching, or of being "up behind" the experience.

A case that illustrates this point somewhat dramatically is that of Margaret, a thirty eight-year old married woman with three children. When Margaret came for therapy, she stated that her mind would not stop, and she feared she was going crazy. She said she felt like her head was "going to blow up." The symptoms she described in scattered fashion included anxiety, depression, paranoia, disturbed sleep, obsessive worrying, homosexual panic, sex fantasies, guilt, grief, anger, and exhaustion.

With such an array of symptoms, we decided to do some testing in order to zero in more specifically on just what the major difficulty was. Sure enough, the test results as well indicated seven varied and seemingly unrelated clinical patterns and syndromes, all eligible for treatment. The question of what to do and where to begin loomed larger than ever. Without an underlying basis that would account for all the symptoms, therapy would at best be a haphazard affair over a long period of time.

In continuing discussions, we asked if she felt she had ever lost her mind. Margaret was quick to respond emphatically, "No." When asked when she was at her worst, whether she had some sense of watching or witnessing herself go through these disturbing episodes, she replied emphatically, "Yes." There seemed to her to be someone up behind all her episodes watching or observing her behavior.

More discussion with Margaret revealed that she frequently was aware that she was dreaming while the dream was actually going on. On several occasions, she heard herself snore while she was sleeping. She also had noticed how on many occasions she seemed to know what was going to happen before it happened and frequently knew when a relative living some distance away was ill or was going to telephone.

Margaret remembered as far back as ninth grade when she was writing "religious poetry" and described herself even then as a seeker after God. She had had a long period of being at peace with herself. She had belonged to a charismatic prayer group for a while and practiced meditation, only to discontinue both because she frequently felt that her mind had stopped and that she was somehow out of her body while meditating. These past few years, however, getting little results from anything she practiced, she had become disenchanted with everything and increasingly sullen.

With what now seemed to be signs of psychological disturbance accompanying the growth of consciousness, we assured Margaret she was not going crazy, but growing sane. This, and an explanation of consciousness, its expansion, and the related mechanics of stress release, provided her with enormous relief. In addition to this intellectual understanding, we taught her the "feeling the body" technique with particular attention to watching her breaths and recommended she get on a "daily routine" as soon as possible. These techniques are described in the last chapter of the book. Margaret responded immediately and very positively to these techniques. In fact, within two weeks she exhibited a sharp reduction in symptoms and became significantly more settled and centered.

What was most interesting to note, too, was that she almost immediately began to practice do-it-yourself therapy quite effectively, and without much guidance at all. She got in touch with her feelings and released much anger and fear. She had numerous psychological insights about herself and in general worked through painful memories and feelings on her own. What was previously unconscious, now seemed very much available to her without digging for it.

Another case, also typical but with different surface symptoms, was that of Charles, a twenty-nine year old male. Charles came for counseling with a variety of symptoms which had recently beset him. He was experiencing self-doubt, discouragement, resentment about his life-style, social inhibition, emotional outbursts of crying and a nagging sense of unfulfillment. He had been involved in a consciousness program for several years, and he had practiced a number of mental and physical techniques with good results. His initial experience with this particular program included deep inner tranquility and bliss, a feeling of knowing everything. In addition, he experienced a profound sense of order and purpose in the world.

He was so appreciative of his initial happiness he decided to share his new-found experience with friends, relatives and others, and attempted to get them to do as he had done. He devoted himself to the pursuit with a great deal of fervor. In the process, he gave up his social life, girlfriend and his quest for money and a good job. He also radically altered his eating and drinking habits so he could begin to live a "pure life." He did all this because he was trying to match his outer life-style to his profound inner experience.

The result of all of this was the deterioration of his outer life, which in turn began to affect his inner life. He was sharply aware of every phase of his discouragement, resentment and inhibitions, watched each mood come and go, yet he was helpless to do anything about it. Inside his mind, he was awake and clear, but outside in his daily activities his life was an unfulfilled mess. He was at a point where he said, "The hell with it all." He negated all of his former aspirations; he doubted the value of his good inner experiences. In fact, he began to wonder if he'd ever really had the experiences.

Most of all, he despaired about his ability to do anything about his conditions. So he resigned himself to "waiting to see what nature had in store for him." He took most of this lying down–literally lying down in bed. We suggested several techniques to Charles, such as intense physical exercise, daily act of the will, and affirmations. By putting these suggestions into action, he quickly rose above his dilemma. His inner experience of peace and happiness came to be matched by outer dynamic and healthy activity.

Now our purpose here is not to keep you in suspense about the techniques we suggest for erasing these severe disturbances. But it is important for you to have a very clear understanding of what is happening to you before you begin to apply techniques of self-help. In fact, this very clear understanding is itself the most important tool you can have in helping yourself go through periods of disturbance. And, specifically, the understanding we would like you to have about Margaret and Charles is the most important thing we have to tell you, because it is pretty much the basis of this entire book.

Although Margaret and Charles went through very troubled periods, they were not really candidates for drugs, hospitalization, or intensive psychotherapy. True, some of the troubled symptoms they experienced were similar to those of persons experiencing mental illness. But the all-important difference is that Margaret and Charles maintained the basic reality of who they were by standing outside and examining their own symptoms. Even though they were playing an unpleasant role, and even though they had no direct control over that role, *still they never lost themselves in the role they were playing.*

On the other hand, truly psychotic, deeply ill persons are not able to tell the difference between themselves and the symptoms; in a sense they become the symptoms. Psychotic persons are by no means detached observers, watching themselves play an unpleasant role. In fact, truly psychotic persons are so overcome and overshadowed by their symptoms that they frequently do not know enough even to seek help from their suffering.

When a person is not aware of his own behavior but becomes fully identified with that behavior, then we can say there is a loss of contact with reality, and this absence from reality is the very hallmark of psychosis. In this sense, awareness is reality, and the absence of awareness is the loss of reality.

In other words, what we are saying is that there sometimes seems to be only a thin boundary between disturbances that accompany the growth of consciousness and real mental illness. Yet the difference is profoundly important. In the case of mental illness, people experience withdrawal from reality, retreating into a world that is imaginary and often incoherent and chaotic. **In the crises that we face along the path toward full potential, we are not withdrawing from reality, but drawing toward reality.** Along with British psychiatrist R. D. Laing and others, we may wonder how many wrong diagnoses were made in the past–how many people were burned at the stake, or confined in mental hospitals for exhibiting symptoms of the growth of consciousness!

Throughout this book we will occasionally refer to behaviors of individuals on the path to enlightenment which resemble the behaviors of mentally ill people. This resemblance is superficial and should never lead us into the dangerous conclusion of confusing enlightenment with insanity or considering insane behavior as a necessary step to full development.

The path to enlightenment, or full development, is full of transitional states, bridges which have to be crossed, and these bridges have to be recognized by all of us as natural results of the growth of consciousness rather than being labeled as insanity.

At the same time, we all need to be very careful not to join the fantasy world of those throughout the ages who have believed that all mental illness is really a higher form of perception and reality. Sometimes this makes for an interesting novel or entertaining movie, but it is definitely fiction and not fact.

Research into the prevention and cure of mental illness still needs to be encouraged and expanded, and our age has seen important strides taken in this direction. Nor are we overlooking the necessity that sometimes individuals who are undergoing a growth of consciousness crisis need to seek professional help when it is necessary. We will discuss this more later, when we deal with the question of when to seek outside help.

However, if you have been looking for a theory which treats the growth of awareness, you have found that ordinary psychology is very limited. The reason for this is simply that ordinary psychology is used to dealing with persons who have accumulated such an abundance of stress in their lives that they are incapable of living a normal life under the strain.

Disturbances that result from over-accumulation of stress generally lead to what we call mental illness.

But as we will see in the next chapter, the problems we experience on the road to full awareness or enlightenment are not the result of increasing accumulation of stress but just the opposite. They are the result of the release of stress. The body and the mind are purifying themselves of stress, sometimes in a faster and more intense way than we know how to handle.

Sometimes the symptoms of a person gathering stress and those of a person releasing stress may appear to be very similar. But there are simple and important differences. First, and most obvious, a person accumulating stress is getting sicker, while a person releasing stress is getting healthier and growing sane.

Furthermore, there is an important difference between the reality experienced by a person continually accumulating stress and the reality of a person releasing stress. A person accumulating stress is less and less able to handle even ordinary reality and in severe cases retreats to a fantasy world of imagination or to drugs and alcohol. On the other hand, as you will see in this book, a person in the process of releasing stress is not retreating from reality, but is advancing toward the experience of the ultimate reality of life, the direct experience of his or her own unlimited potential.

In general, psychologists have focused on the mechanics of stress accumulation rather than stress release. Nor has psychology generally recognized the experience of the growth of consciousness. Fortunately, there are signs that psychology is entering a new era and is beginning to consider these missing factors. The distinguished psychologist, Carl Rogers, has said,

Perhaps in the coming generation of younger psychologists, there may be a few who will dare to investigate the possibility that there is a lawful reality which is not open to our five senses; a reality in which present, past and future are intermingled, in which space is not a barrier and time has disappeared; a reality which can be perceived and known only when we are passively receptive rather than actively bent on knowing. It is one of the most exciting challenges posed to psychology.

We are witnessing the beginnings of that future. In the new age, psychology and other healing arts will need to focus on wellness at least as much as they do on illness. Almost all techniques of psychological diagnosis are based on accumulation of stress and are therefore oriented toward producing a diagnosis of mental illness. Until now, psychologists who have tried to measure super-normal people have been the rare exception. But there is no good reason that the same intelligence and creativity which have gone into acquiring reliable measurements of mental illness cannot go into acquiring reliable measurements of mental wellness.

In just the same way that the overwhelming majority of psychological tests and measurements do not apply to levels of increasing wellness, neither do the overwhelming majority of therapies. The reason is very simple. There are a number of different techniques of psychotherapy, but most of them have one thing in common. They share the belief that psychological disturbances are caused by unresolved problems on the deeper level of the mind.

According to this belief, these deep problems occasionally surface into our conscious awareness and into our daily lives, and when this happens we are unable to handle them. Therefore, most psychological techniques tend to probe the "unconscious" or deeper levels of the mind in order to attack the underlying cause. There could be many different paths to the unconscious, but the goal is the same–to expose a deeper level of the mind so that deep-rooted stresses or traumas can be unearthed.

But these techniques are simply not relevant to those of you undergoing a growth crisis. Such a crisis occurs from already being in the process of releasing a great deal of debris from the past. So what we need at these points in life is not to go back and bring up to the surface even more old garbage; rather, we need specific programs which will help us stabilize the gains we have made and prepare us for the next step in our journey.

To put it simply, what you need after a great unearthing or upheaval is some smoothing out, not more upheaval. For this reason we also need to be cautious about the overuse of programs which will intensify the release of deep stress. Many mind-body techniques of self-improvement, such as body work, meditation, or relaxation, tend to uncover deep layers of stress in a natural and peaceful way.

If you are already experiencing discomfort from the release of deep stress, over-application of self-improvement techniques without adequate supervision under the guidance of an experienced teacher can produce even more turbulence. For those of us experiencing growth crises, the aim of any program is to help us continue to grow, but in a calmer and smoother manner. We hope that is what this book will help you to do.

Two
Stress Release

We said in Chapter One that the disturbances which accompany the growth of consciousness are due to the release of stress. In this chapter, we will explore for you the essential mechanics of how stress is released.

What you need to know, first of all, is that stress is essentially a disorder. Any time there is an imbalance in the body-mind, we can call this imbalance "stress." It may be a misalignment of your spine; it may be chemicals in your blood which indicate a high level of anxiety or some irrational or negative thoughts; or, it may be barely traceable electrical misfirings in your nervous system. However it shows itself, stress is unnatural and does not belong in your body-mind.

In whatever form stress may be stored in our body-mind, it has probably come about through our own activities–not through some accident of "fate" or "misfortune." Whenever we face a pressure which we cannot handle, it will cause stress to be stored in our minds or bodies. It doesn't matter whether the cause is physical—like over-fatigue—or mental–like a terrible crisis in our lives; the end result is an accumulation of pressure and a harmful effect on our nervous system. We can say that on the physical level, stress is stored someplace deep in the nervous system, and on the mental level, someplace deep in the unconscious.

Since stress is unnatural and doesn't belong in the body-mind, the body-mind is naturally inclined to rid itself of this unwanted visitor. Our bodies do not have to be **forced** to throw off stress. All our bodies really want is to be **allowed** to get rid of stress. The reason for this is simply that it is the natural tendency of the body to be well. Nevertheless, when your body or mind throw off stress, you often feel very uncomfortable. Sometimes you can feel as uncomfortable throwing off stress as you do when you take on stress.

We want to discuss what happens to you when you release stress, because this release is what causes the psychological disturbances accompanying the growth of consciousness. But in order for you to understand what happens when stress is released, you need to know a little bit about how stress is taken on in the first place.

As we have already mentioned, any pressure or experience which puts an overload on the body is stress. There could be thousands of examples. They include doing strenuous physical labor beyond the capability of the body, so that the body suffers from severe exhaustion; going without sleep for a long period of time; listening to deafening noise; drinking large amounts of alcohol; or taking drugs or other harmful substances which have a profound effect on our nervous systems. These examples are all physical in nature and their harmful effect on the body is fairly obvious.

It is also true that there are numerous powerful psychological events which can affect your body in a similar way. For example, the death of someone we love does not affect our own physical body directly, but the sorrow that we feel may cause deep physical stress to the point where we are actually ill. Another example would be excessive worry that a project in which we are involved will not succeed. Even if the project does end up succeeding, the worry will have caused us stress. All of these stress–full activities have a physical effect because each of them, although mental in nature, leaves an impression on the body.

Our human nature tends to blame other people or "the situation" for the stress which we are experiencing. But this is wrong. What causes stress is our irrational perception of, or our inability to react to, a situation. As an ancient Roman philosopher said, "People are not really upset by other people, situations or things, but by the way they look at other people, situations, and things." For example, if we were alone with some harmless snake in a cage, you might faint with fear. But a person with knowledge about snakes would be a master of the situation and would feel no fear at all. So, how we look at it, or our inability to successfully cope with a situation, is what makes that situation stressful. For some people, just to get out of bed in the morning is an impossibly stressful situation.

When we take on stress, it is often because we have some bodily weakness or our minds are clouded and confused. Because we are in a weak or confused state, it's difficult to tell how deep an impression a particular stress makes. Since you are obviously not at your best when you take on stress, it could be that a relatively natural or seemingly simple event makes a deep impression which you carry with you for a long period of time. Sometimes you find yourself thinking back to something that happened to you an hour, a day, or even a week ago, and you suddenly find yourself terrified. On the other hand, you might find yourself in what seems to be a very terrifying situation–and then an hour later you are thinking, "How silly of me to be so frightened at something so trivial." What seemed a little while ago to be so earth-shaking left hardly an impression at all.

The factor that really determines how deep the impression will be is our state of awareness–or state of consciousness– at the time of the occurring stress. To a fully aware, healthy, enlightened individual, very little, if anything, is stressful. To a dull, unaware, unhealthy individual, anything–the smallest noise, or the smallest disappointment–is liable to cause stress. In the ancient scriptures of India, it is said that impressions made upon an aware and enlightened person are like lines drawn on water–they leave no trace at all. But impressions made upon a dull, unaware state of mind are like lines chiseled on rock. **The real difference lies in who is receiving the impression, not in the situation that causes the impression.**

Much of the surface stress we experience during our daily activity is released when we sleep or dream. But deeper stress has a way of accumulating over time, and accumulated stress has a disastrous effect on our bodies. This effect is seen in the array of what are called "psychosomatic" illnesses. These are illnesses where we experience very definite physical symptoms, but where the real causes are psychological. Common examples would be tension headaches, ulcers, high blood pressure and even certain forms of heart disease. Restlessness, fatigue, indigestion and backaches also frequently have psychological causes.

Sometimes stress can leave a deep impression on our minds without noticeably affecting our bodies. Sigmund Freud and other great pioneers in the field of psychology discovered that the psychological problems we face as adults have their origins in unreleased stresses that we experienced as young children. Freud called these stresses "traumas." When those stresses are repressed, they tend to collect in our unconscious minds, and then they surface in unpredictable ways when we are adults.

In short, stress wreaks havoc on both our minds and bodies. More and more, modern medicine is coming to recognize the stress that we accumulate, through unaware minds and bad physical habits, as the principal cause of illness or disease. The meaning of disease is simply **dis–ease,** or lack of ease, and it is stress that causes this lack.

When we consider that stress is essentially disorder, then it becomes even clearer that stress is the major cause of all mental and physical diseases. In every disease that we encounter, something is disordered, out of place, inappropriate, or disorganized. Certainly the class of disease we call psychosomatic falls into this category. In these cases, there is an over-accumulation of tension which disrupts and disorganizes the body's natural tendency to remain healthy, and results in localized pain somewhere in the body.

In the same way, disorder is also the cause of everything from cancer to mental diseases such as schizophrenia. Cancer is a runaway growth that is out of place in the body. The principal characteristic of schizophrenia is a disorder of the normal thinking process. The electrical brain wave activity of schizophrenics is also marked by abnormal patterns. "Disorderly conduct" applies not only to delinquents and criminals but also to our organs, nerves, thoughts, and feelings.

Now, whenever disorder enters your body, then your body has a natural tendency to want to rid itself of this disorder. You are not always successful, of course, but still the tendency is always there. Whenever you get a splinter under the skin, you can watch the process in action. First, there is an inflammation around the foreign object, and then the object is gradually pushed out. It happens by itself–not because we make it happen or because we want it to happen.

The same process occurs with all the stresses of life. Our minds and bodies are continually attempting to rid themselves of these stresses. When stresses are unstressed, there is bound to be some discomfort, sometimes similar (but not necessarily) to the discomfort we experienced when the stress went in. This is a simple but profoundly important fact for you to be aware of.

It means that when you are unstressing, you need to be aware of what is happening and make a practical effort to make the process easier and smoother. If you don't know that you are unstressing, or you are told by someone that you "need help," you could very easily take measures that would actually prevent your releasing the stress. Unfortunately, this happens all too frequently to too many people and is largely due to the fact that psychologists and doctors know very little about the release of stress. Psychology has tended to treat every disturbance as a symptom of sickness, whereas, in fact, such disturbances may be signs of wellness!

At this point, you may be ready to ask a very practical question. Is there a good way to tell the difference between those occasions when we are taking on stress and those occasions when we are throwing off stress? No and yes. No, there is no absolutely hard and fast rule. In both the taking on and throwing off of stress, our minds and bodies are disturbed; therefore we are not always able to know and analyze the difference. And we cannot tell the difference by the amount of discomfort we are experiencing. It could be that the throwing off of stress often seems more uncomfortable than the taking on of the same kind of stress.

But yes, there is a pretty good rule of thumb that will help you to know the difference between the times you are taking in stress and the times you are releasing stress. Examine your life. Are there obvious situations which would tend to make you irritable, depressed, tired, or even sick? Situations such as poor eating habits, an unpleasant experience with a loved one, overwork, lack of sleep? In these cases, there are obvious causes of stress.

However, if there are no obvious signs, and if you have to ask yourself the question, "What is it that is making me feel this way?" then we have an obvious case for unstressing. If you have never asked this question, and it would never occur to you to do so, then you are probably not unstressing. But if you feel for the most part that you are avoiding stressful situations, and yet the psychological disturbances persist, then unstressing is a possible cause.

It is mostly for these individuals, those experiencing intense unstressing, that this book is written. These are the people who, either through the mere passing of time or because of a specific consciousness-raising technique, are experiencing periods where large quantities of stress are being released and temporarily creating mental or even physical disturbances. The mere passage of time can sometimes cause you to unstress heavily just because it is the natural tendency of our body and mind to be healthy and therefore throw off stress. Whenever the mind and body have a chance to do so— and we can hardly ever predict exactly when–you may throw off a particularly burdensome stress.

But in today's society, unstressing is particularly important not so much because of the passage of time but because of the widespread participation in human potential and growth movements. And this is because any technique which you may practice that facilitates human growth, facilitates at the same time the throwing off of stress. Unstressing and growth–especially rapid growth–are two sides of the same coin.

You cannot go forward unless you release the past. So any legitimate technique of growth or purification will cause you to release stress, and this includes meditation, diet, massage, certain forms of psychotherapy, fasting, biofeedback–even prayer. The acceleration of the growth of consciousness through such techniques causes the psychological disturbances which accompany the growth of consciousness.

Whenever you experience these disturbances, it is generally not possible and not even desirable, to know which stress is being released. We may compare the process to throwing out garbage. Much of psychology today is based upon the idea that in order to throw out the old garbage in your life you have to get reacquainted with it before you can get rid of it. "Oh, there is the rind of the melon that I had two days ago;" (i.e., "Here's the stress that I experienced 20 years ago as a child when I got lost and was terrified.") But in older, more traditional techniques of growth such as meditation, which have surfaced again in modern times, it isn't necessary to encounter and recount every past stress in your life before you get rid of it.

Anyway, even if you wanted to know what particular stresses in your nervous system are being released, it is not always possible. When you are unstressing heavily, it could be that many small quantities are being released at the same time, thus adding up to what seems to be one large quantity. Or it could be that just one strong or very deep stress is being released.

One way of understanding the mechanics of how this happens is to visualize our nervous systems as having many different levels, from surface to very deep. If one strong bubble were initiated from the bottom of the pond, it would travel upward and noticeably disturb the surface. But if many small bubbles were initiated together, close to the surface, they could cause the same amount of disturbance. Looking at the pond from the surface, we can't really tell exactly what caused the disturbance.

You release stress in much the same way. Perhaps in your childhood you suffered a very deep trauma–some violence, some fear, some rejection. This trauma has made its impression deep within the nervous system, so deep that it is beyond your level of conscious awareness. It is deposited in that level of the mind which we call the unconscious. When your nervous system begins to become normal–either through the passage of time or through a particular technique of normalization such as diet, massage, meditation, etc., then the path becomes cleared for this stress to be released. The impact of the release is bound to be disturbing. In the release you will experience some of the same emotional insecurity and physical instability as when you took on the stress.

When you release numerous small stresses, like the many bubbles near the surface of the pond, the impact of the disturbances may be very similar to the release of the one large trauma. Examples of small stresses could be experiences like over-stimulation of the senses through exposure to loud noises, a discomfort which could result from being trapped in a large, pushy crowd, or just an argument with a friend.

But the important thing for you to remember is that it doesn't make any real difference whether the stresses are large or small, where they come from, or why you sustained them. Because the symptoms all fall into the same general categories, then the measure which we will recommend to you will apply no matter what. Of course, there may be some intellectual insight and satisfaction in knowing exactly where your stresses come from. But generally, such an examination will lead you backward in your life to a dead end. It is so tedious and time-consuming that you will end up spending more energy on uncovering the past than on living a fulfilled life, here and now. The only real advantage of having insight into the cause of stress is to avoid taking on any more similar stress in your life.

Remember this–if you are experiencing a wave of heavy unstressing, it's only a temporary state, just as the wavy surface of a calm pond will return to its natural state. When you are unstressing, the waves of stress are being weakened and your nervous system is returning to a smoother, more stabilized state. Unstressing is definitely a temporary state, and our concern here is to make the transition as smooth as possible.

We will be offering various methods to achieve this transition, but one of the most important is what we have been offering all along, and that is a clear understanding of what is happening to you. If you really understand precisely what is happening at these points in the development of your life, then that understanding, by itself, will prevent your falling into certain well known traps, such as reliance upon tranquilizers or lengthy and unnecessary analysis of your problems.

In other words, if you are interested in your own growth and development, then it is necessary to have a clear understanding of the disturbances which might accompany this growth. If you fail to achieve this understanding, you could start treating the disturbing symptoms as if they themselves were the disease. If you do that, you are mistakenly treating yourself like a sick person rather than as an individual who is rapidly developing into a whole, healthy person.

For a completely clear understanding of what is happening to us, it is important to remember (and it is worth repeating) that "For every state of body, there is a corresponding state of mind." We have been referring to the nervous system as the site where stress is stored, and from where stress is released. But because stress is released on a physical level, then it must also be released on a mental level. You will be able to relate to this in a very personal way if you can remember how easy it is to be morbid and depressed whenever you get physically ill. On the other hand, when you begin to recover physically, then you seem to have a brighter outlook on life. It is also our everyday experience that when we get angry, our muscles stiffen, our blood pressure rises, and our hearts pound and beat faster.

In the light of our own personal experience, and in the light of modern scientific discoveries, there is absolutely no room for the separation of mind and body. Sophisticated scientific instrumentation gives ample evidence to show that even subtle physical processes are accompanied by corresponding mental states. For example, the electroencephalogram (EEG) measures electrical activity of the brain which corresponds to a very calm and relaxed state of mind. The Galvanic Skin Response (GSR), used in lie detector tests, uses skin resistance and can record an underlying nervousness and stress, even though all appears to be calm on the surface. In the same way, the release of stress may sometimes seem to be more physical, sometimes more mental, but physical and mental unstressing are two sides of the same coin.

Another important way to understand the release of stress is to see it in terms of the growth of consciousness. The process of the release of stress is just a stage in growth. This shouldn't surprise us if we think about the fact that many patterns of growth in our lives follow the same procedure. For example, psychological research has shown that the process of learning is not continuous, but occurs with rises, falls, and plateaus. In any process of psychological growth, a fall backward can actually be a natural and necessary step. This is also true in the growth of consciousness.

As we proceed toward the fullness of life, there are definite stages. Sometimes we seem to take a big step backward by exposing ourselves to very stressful situations and taking on new stresses which eventually have to be released. Sometimes we move forward in leaps and bounds, avoiding stressful situations and following daily regimens which lead to better health and mental clarity. Sometimes we seem to be in slow periods where we are learning to apply the gains we have made to our daily activity.

And sometimes, even without our planning to, we move ahead so quickly that all hell seems to break loose. This is the stage which is our concern and which we are explaining here. When we find ourselves in this stage of growth, we are undergoing rapid purification, and the changes are jarring. These changes are really periods of rapid adjustment where the mind and body are getting used to more evolved states.

Our minds and bodies can actually get addicted to stress in the same way that an alcoholic is addicted to liquor. When liquor is taken away from the alcoholic, it takes a period of greater vulnerability and uneasy adjustment to get used to a more normal state of mind and body. And in the same way, when you remove stress from your life, your mind and body can actually be jarred rather disturbingly into a more normal state.

Of course, the positive side of all of this is that when these changes occur, you are becoming a truly normal and natural person–normal in the sense that you are returning to your true nature. One of the most uplifting things you can do for yourself is to realize that the release of stress is a transition on the way to the ultimate goal of enlightenment or actualization of full potential.

It is not our intention here to pass judgment on, or recommend, any particular means of stress release. But it is important for you to understand why many techniques of self-growth and improvement are more effective than others in counteracting stress. The reason is very simple. We have said that stress is disorder, so it is reasonable to conclude that any technique or process which introduces order will be the enemy of stress.

Now, it is your everyday experience that anything which is disordered is unsettled, always changing, and moving in a turbulent and random way. When we don't feel right, we often say we're "disturbed" or "agitated" or "unable to settle down." Orderliness in your mind and body increases as you are able to settle down, and change and movement decrease. What this means simply is that a body at rest is more ordered than a body that is not at rest. This is the reason that deep rest or relaxation techniques such as meditation, breathing exercises, and biofeedback have been found to be effective in reducing and preventing stress. The reason is that such techniques allow your nervous system to come closer to a completely settled state of mind.

This completely settled state of mind has been called pure awareness or transcendental consciousness. To "transcend" means to go beyond; and in this state you have gone beyond waking, sleeping, or dreaming to a state of perfect order and rest. Any worthwhile technique of self-improvement must have as its goal the uncovering of your basic core–transcendental consciousness–and allow the perfect order and tranquility of this state of consciousness to permeate your whole mind and body. This is the stated aim of such popular centering techniques as meditation, Tai Chi, Yoga, and biofeedback. Perfect orderliness is always there inside you waiting to be uncovered.

Of course, there are many techniques of self-improvement besides relaxation techniques, such as certain forms of psychotherapy, but these also have as their goal to strip away the disorder and agitation on the outside in order to reveal the order and calm on the inside. Regardless of the means or the technique, the goal is to experience the internal state of deep rest and no stress.

The more order, the less disorder. The more you experience deep rest on the inside, the more stress is released. And as more stress is released, you grow in consciousness. Therefore, deep rest is the basis for the purification of consciousness. Your personal evolution proceeds in steps of rest and activity. It is rest, or non-movement, which is the basis of activity. This is the paradox upon which all growth is based. Deep rest, or deep calm, produces the right condition for purification or the elimination of stress, and therefore for the growth of consciousness.

If rest is one step on the road of progress, the next step is activity. If rest eliminates stress and pacifies your nervous system so that you can gain increased awareness, then activity stabilizes, integrates and allows you to enjoy the gains you have made. Just as in walking, there has to be one foot on the ground and one foot moving, so too all growth, including the growth of consciousness, proceeds in steps of rest and activity.

Whenever you are growing, it's like moving from one place to another. The new place is better than the old place, but even so, in any move you make, you need to accustom yourself to your new surroundings. At least you have to look around to see where you are before you feel comfortable. Your first reaction to the unfamiliar surroundings might be disturbing. But as you begin to act, you feel more at home. Only activity–not thinking, brooding or anything else–can do this.

After you feel integrated with your new surroundings and after more rest, you may be ready to move on again. How much progress you are able to make in your next move depends on how deep the rest is that you get and how much you have been able to stabilize and integrate your previous gains.

Three
Consciousness

In this chapter we want to further clarify what we mean by consciousness because, as we have said, full understanding of yourself and what is happening to you is the most important therapy you can enjoy. Much of what we are saying here has been thought by many to be in the realm of deep philosophy. But consciousness is not really an esoteric subject. It is explainable according to scientific principles as well as common experience; and for most of us it is definitely within the realm of understanding and experience.

First of all, in order to understand consciousness in its fullest sense you need to realize that consciousness has a wide range. It is just like any physical object, for example, a flower. A flower has a surface which is very obvious. Look at a rose. It has a certain color, a specific size and definite shape. But the rose has a less obvious, more subtle aspect which you are not able to see with the naked eye. It has a chemical structure, molecular structure, atomic structure; and at the basis of the atomic structure is the field of pure energy which underlies all of matter.

Consciousness is just like a rose. It has an obvious side to it and a less obvious, very subtle aspect as well. We said earlier that the deepest most subtle layer of consciousness is what we call transcendental consciousness, or the Self, because to transcend means to go beyond. Transcendental consciousness goes beyond the surface activity of your mind and is the very deepest layer of yourself. It has also been called pure consciousness, pure awareness and by many other names. Maybe these names are not familiar to you but that does not really matter. Many people have never heard of these names and yet have still experienced this subtle state of awareness. And still more people have experienced transcendental consciousness without even remembering it.

Transcendental consciousness is the foundation for all of our mental activity–the basis of thought itself. Imagine it to be like a backdrop of a stage. Different players–the different roles that you play in life–act on the stage in different scenes, but the backdrop always remains the same. Or you may think of transcendental consciousness as a movie screen. Different images are continually flashed on it but the screen itself never changes. It is the most profound part of you—the part that is always you through all of your different roles and activities. That is why it is called the Self.

The idea of transcendental consciousness or a permanent backdrop inside of us for all our thoughts and behaviors once seemed very abstract and philosophical. But today many of us are beginning to experience this state of consciousness as a living reality, and it is vitally important that we begin to understand its practical application–what it does for us in our daily lives

To help you see more clearly what transcendental consciousness is, we will explain it in light of those states of consciousness with which you are already familiar. The familiar states of consciousness are waking, dreaming, and sleeping. If transcendental consciousness is the permanent backdrop against which you play out your life, then you can consider waking, dreaming and sleeping as minor backdrops. These are minor backdrops because you are never continuously awake, asleep, or dreaming.

The presence or absence of thoughts and awareness can be used as the two major ways of determining which state of consciousness you are experiencing. If you have awareness and thoughts going on at the same time—that is, you are thinking and you know it—then you are awake. If both thoughts and awareness are absent—then you are in deep sleep. If your deep sleep is interrupted by thoughts, which you are not aware of, (at least while you are having them) then you are dreaming. And finally, there is the fourth state—transcendental consciousness. This state is marked by the presence of awareness and the absence of thoughts. This is the reason why this state of consciousness is often called pure consciousness or pure awareness—because it is pure awareness in and of itself without thoughts.

We can put all of these four states of consciousness into perspective through a simple diagram.

THOUGHTS

A W A R E N E S S		Yes	No
	Yes	Waking Consciousness	Transcendental Consciousness
	No	Dream Consciousness	Sleep Consciousness

Now we will look at each of these states of consciousness a bit more closely, beginning with waking. It is our
everyday experience that when we are awake, some mental
activity–thought–is taking place within our minds. There may
also be some physical activity such as talking, running, or
walking. But the major distinguishing feature of being awake
is not physical activity. After all, some people talk in their
sleep; some people even walk in their sleep. So it is not the
talking or the walking or any other activity which determines
whether you are awake, but rather the thoughts that accompany these activities. Because whenever you perform an
action, whether it is playing a musical instrument, or jogging,
or deciding which shoes to wear in the morning, there is at
least some level of thought which precedes and accompanies
the experience. All of your speech, your feelings, your
decisions, and your actions are really projections of your
thoughts.

Thus, we can agree that thought is a necessary ingredient of being awake. But thought by itself is not the only
necessary ingredient. In order to experience thought or its
projection into speech, feeling and actions, you at least need
to be aware. If you are not aware of your thoughts then you
are dreaming or you are acting unconsciously–as if you are
sleep-walking. But if we are aware, and the mind is active
with thoughts, then we are awake. Thus waking can be
defined as the activity or vibration of thought against the
backdrop of awareness.

For very good reasons, we generally think of sleep as the
opposite of waking. And this is because in sleep there is
neither thought nor awareness. You may say, "Last night I
slept poorly," or "I slept peacefully." But, in fact, this is
something you know when you wake up, not while you are

actually asleep, because while you are asleep you are unaware. You are not conscious of yourself, nor of what you are doing, nor of your surroundings. In fact, in one sense it is better to call this state just sleep rather than sleep consciousness, because we are not conscious of sleeping while we are doing so.

The third state of consciousness with which all of us are familiar is dreaming. In this state there are thoughts without awareness. Described in this way, dreaming may seem a very unusual experience. But of course it is a very common experience, and research shows that all of us spend a good part of every night dreaming. We may, and often do, have dreams that seem very far removed from reality. We find ourselves in unfamiliar places, saying strange things; and yet while we are dreaming it all seems very real. Only when we begin to awaken from a dream, as in a nightmare or the last twenty minutes of sleep during the morning, do we have any real awareness. And only at that point do we know that what we experienced was only a dream.

The actual thoughts or images which you have during a dream are connected more with your unconscious mind than they are with your awareness. That is why if you want to consistently remember your dreams, you almost always have to write them down upon awakening. Otherwise, before you begin to know it, the dream which seemed so real has slipped back into your unconscious—a storehouse of past impressions of which you are seldom sharply aware.

These three states of consciousness—waking, dreaming and sleeping—are the familiar"everyday" states of consciousness, the minor backdrops against which we play out our lives. Behind these three backdrops is the major backdrop which we have called transcendental consciousness.

In human history there have always been long periods of time when the fourth state of consciousness has been thought to be mystical or philosophical, something far removed from the experience of ordinary people. And then there have been periods when transcendental consciousness has been very much within the realm of common experience for people from all walks of life. We seem now to be entering such an age, when the fourth state of consciousness can be explained in simple and scientific terms. When a simple explanation of the fourth state of consciousness can appeal to a cross-section of people, it is because this state of consciousness has become familiar to them through their own experience.

We said earlier that transcendental consciousness is most simply described as a state of **pure** awareness. If we say that consciousness in general is like a movie screen on which we usually see flashing either waking, dreaming, or sleeping, then we can say that **pure** awareness is the screen itself, without anything flashing on it. Most of us get so accustomed to the images flashing on the screen of the mind that we forget about the screen itself, but the screen is always there. It is like a silent witness to all of our activities. Because it is our true nature, that part of us that never changes, it has often, as we said earlier, been referred to as the Self with a capital "S."

When this Self becomes part of our living experience, so that we are able to enjoy its great potential, then this condition is called Self-Realization. This means simply that pure awareness, or the Self, has been made real–no longer just a vague and hidden background for all of our thoughts and actions but a living reality whose power we are able to actually experience in our everyday life.

The psychologist Abraham Maslow has said,

> We have, each of us, an essential biologically-based inner nature, which is to some degree 'natural,' intrinsic, given and in a certain limited sense unchangeable or at least unchanging... It is possible to discover this inner nature scientifically and to discover what it is like.

We are no longer in an age when pure awareness needs to be the secret possession of a few mystics who live in monasteries, forests, or caves. In our scientific age it is proper and very revealing to examine transcendental consciousness in the cold light of science.

The pathway for the scientific study of transcendental consciousness is through the principle we have already stated, that what happens in the mind also happens in the body. That is why a scientist in another room, with the proper instrumentation hooked up to our bodies, should be able to tell whether we are waking, dreaming, or sleeping. Some of the measurements which would help the scientists to determine which state of consciousness we are experiencing would include electrical activity of the brain, metabolic activity of the body, oxygen consumption, skin resistance, and the rapid eye movement (REM) which occurs during dreaming.

The same principle applies to transcendental consciousness. If this is a distinct and important state of consciousness, then there must be a measurable and corresponding state of body. And in fact this is exactly what numerous scientific studies have begun to show to be true–that when a person directly experiences the state of pure awareness, the body acts in a very definite way.

Since the state of pure awareness, or transcendental consciousness, is our own true Self and the basis of all other states of consciousness, it is to be expected that the corresponding state of body would be very restful, healthful, and life-giving. The scientific findings about transcendental consciousness, (done originally on Buddhist monks and most recently and extensively on people who practice popular meditation techniques such as Transcendental Meditation) do, in fact, indicate a high degree of life-supporting activity taking place in the body during the experiences of this state of consciousness.

For example, recent experiments have shown a healthy coherence in the electrical activity between the left and right hemispheres of the brain. Since it is now believed that each hemisphere of the brain controls different facets of our personality, (the analytic and verbal on the left side and the synthetic and spatial on the right side) more coherence between the two hemispheres would indicate a more balanced personality. Other studies examining meditative (or deeply relaxed) states have shown decreases in heart rate and blood pressure which indicate a degree of relaxation, even greater than what is experienced during sleep. When the mind returns to its own source, it is natural that the body will experience an extraordinary amount of vitality and rejuvenation.

Other benefits that occur with a state of very deep rest and relaxation are: reduction of certain chemicals in the blood which indicate stress, faster reaction time, sharper perceptions, better concentration, decreased anxiety and depression, and decreased alcohol and drug abuse.

If you look at all four states of consciousness you will realize that each of them is essential in your life. First of all, you obviously need to be awake, for it is the waking state that allows you to experience and enjoy life. If you spent your life in sleep, or in a coma, then you would consider that life to be a waste. You also know from experience that you need to sleep; it is not just a luxury which you can take or leave. In fact, it has been a common device of torture in prison camps to deny a person sleep. After a number of days without sleep, the prisoner experiences such fatigue and exhaustion that he quickly breaks down.

Now let us take a look at the dream state. Until recently, it was not even clear that the dream state was a separate state of consciousness. Modern scientific experiments have shown the dreaming is, in fact, a separate state and that like waking and sleeping, it seems to be quite necessary for human survival. Because it is possible to know through rapid eye movement (REM) when a person is beginning to dream, experimenters have been able to awaken a person just at this point and thus deprive a person of dreaming. The experiments have been very revealing. After a few days and nights without dreams, a person begins to exhibit signs of severe anxiety and sensory disturbances and psychotic-like behavior.

The reason for this is that dreams are a way of releasing stress during sleep. The release of physical stress that we experience during sleep is accompanied by a corresponding sequence of thoughts–a dream. If we block dreams, then we are preventing a necessary release of stress. The fact that dreams are a way of releasing stress may be part of the reason why it is difficult to analyze dreams. A dream is often a chaotic mixture of different stresses with no coherent thread running through it.

While dreaming, sleeping, and waking are all necessary parts of life, the one which we value most, of course, is waking. It is when we are awake that we enjoy real growth in life. And we dream and sleep in order to make the waking state comfortable, not vice-versa. Moreover, it is when we are awake that we are able to make the conscious decision to release stress, or in more negative moments, to accumulate more stress.

In turn, ultimate happiness in the waking state depends upon how firmly we are anchored to our deepest Self, transcendental consciousness. Without this anchor, we float aimlessly through life. So we live to enjoy the waking state, and this enjoyment depends on how much the waking state reflects our deepest core.

Individuals are essentially personalities who act or behave in the waking state. Therefore, it is important that each aspect or component of our personality–or the total of all that makes us individual–is grounded in transcendental consciousness. We will proceed from outer to inner, gross to subtle, and you will see that any part of your personality is capable of reflecting your most inner Self, transcendental consciousness.

We begin with the aspect of ourselves which is potentially the farthest removed from transcendental consciousness. This is the grossest or most outward aspect of ourselves–the body. Our bodies are capable of acting from purely physical needs and desires–on a purely mechanical level. In this case, when the body is disconnected from its own source, transcendental consciousness, it will tend to be unhealthy and unbalanced.

On the other hand, to the extent that the body does reflect the energy and the order of transcendental consciousness, then to that extent it will be healthy and vibrant. A whole person is a person whose body is integrated with his deepest layers of consciousness; and based upon this notion, a new type of medicine called "holistic medicine" has sprung up.

Subtler than the body are the senses, which produce the experience of sight, hearing, taste, touch and smell. These are characteristic of any higher animal, not just mankind.

Subtler than the senses and more characteristically human is the mechanism of perception. The senses give us just the basic raw data, for example, the sight of a bunch of sticks protruding from the ground. But perception tells us that the sticks are a certain height, a specific color, and extend to a certain length over the ground. Perception gives some meaning to the raw data that we get through our senses.

Subtler than the mechanics of perception is what we call the intellect (or discriminating component). The intellect says to you, "Those white sticks rising from the ground are not just there by chance. Someone put them there to make a fence. If I want to get to the other side, maybe I should look for a gate." Accompanying the intellect is the will, that is, the decision to act. The will takes its direction from the intellect. The intellect says, "These are not just sticks rising from the ground for no purpose. They are a fence." The will says, "All right, if this is a fence, then I'll find a way to get to the other side."

But what really motivates us to decide one thing over another is a layer of personality even deeper than the intellect—and this is the emotions or feelings. Besides the negative emotions of fear, anger, and guilt which motivate behavior, there are positive motivators as well. For example, your intellect may tell you, "This person is in need," but the emotions give rise to the feelings of sympathy and compassion which make us want to help our friend in need. So "will" is actually affected by both your emotions and intellect—knowing what to do and feeling motivated to do it.

An even deeper combination of emotion and intellect is what we call "intuition." Intuition is feeling the "truth" or "rightness" of something on a deep emotional level. You may "feel" that you should make a particular investment or that a particular relationship is just not right for you. Your intellect then comes up with some pretty good reasons with which to support these feelings. But really, it is the gut-level, unanalyzed insight which has motivated your decision.

Repeatedly correct intuitions are the mark of a creative person, whether it is an artist choosing the right color on canvas, a business person choosing the right investment, or a mother deciding what is best for her baby. If your emotions are at a very sensitive and finely tuned level, then they are able to draw their power from the energy source itself, transcendental consciousness. At this point, your intuitions are a lot more than just hunches; they are likely to be profound insights which guide you to a more fulfilling life.

Emotions or feelings are a very deep aspect of our personality. Recognizing and accepting our emotions, understanding their source and direction, consciously choosing a life-supporting role for them in our lives—these are the hallmarks of a highly evolved person.

Beneath the level of emotions, there is still one more major layer before we reach transcendental consciousness. That layer is the "ego," our sense of personal identity, or "self concept." Self concept, or the thoughts we have about our self, is synonymous with the ego. The ego, or the sense of "I"-ness, seems to be with us always. Emotions may change. When you feel, "I am glad," or "I am sad," the gladness and sadness may come and go. But the "I" remains at the bottom of your moods, and throughout the changes in your life. Because the ego, or sense of "I," seems to be always there, as the basis of our actions, it is sometimes confused with transcendental consciousness.

Because of this confusion, learning to discriminate between the small self of the ego and the large Self of transcendental consciousness has been seen traditionally in ancient philosophy as the ultimate test of true wisdom. Enlightenment is when we completely know and experience that we are much more than just the ego. The ego is limited by the boundaries of our own individuality. The Self or transcendental consciousness is the unbounded field within us which gives rise to individual boundaries, but which is in itself unlimited.

Confusion between your small self and your big Self is ignorance–the opposite of wisdom or enlightenment. When we spend our lives experiencing only our own individuality–our own ego–then simply by definition our lives are lived in boundaries. Those people who live in boundaries waste a great deal of energy protecting and defending those boundaries. Why? Because they mistakenly feel that the boundaries are all that they have.

On the other hand, those people who understand and experience that they are really more than just their own bounded egos do not need to spend energy defending their little boundaries. This is the state of enlightenment, and people in this state are truly liberated, because, among other things, they do not need to engage in ego-defensive behavior to protect their own territory.

Of course, even liberated people retain their own unique individuality, but this individuality is like a wave on an ocean. The ocean is transcendental consciousness and the ego is the wave. If you believe you are only the wave, then you might worry about losing your identity to the ocean. But if you know that you are really the ocean and the wave is just your own individual expression of the ocean, then you will be liberated from the false fear of having to protect your own little boundaries.

Your body and any dimension of your personality can be reduced to a subtler, quieter, and more harmonious level, and when this happens you are in a favorable position to go beyond or "transcend" that subtle level and experience the subtlest and most profound layer, transcendental consciousness. All it really requires is to reduce the usual turbulence of activity in any dimension to a quiet and orderly state of little or no activity.

For example, it is possible to bring the body to a level of very deep rest and order where the nervous system is functioning smoothly and harmoniously. In this state, your senses are very sharp, and your perception can be activated and clarified at very subtle layers. When this happens, you see the world in a truly different way–as deeply harmonious and bathed in radiance.

The great scientist, Albert Einstein, was thinking of such perceptions when he said, "There are moments when one feels free from one's own identification with human limitations and inadequacies. At such moments, one imagines that one stands on some spot of a small planet, gazing in amazement at the cold yet profoundly moving beauty of the eternal, the unfathomable."

In the same way that your perception can be brought to a very subtle and profound level, so too can your intellect. Your intellect may be sharpened so that you can learn to discriminate between appearance and reality and therefore perform all of your actions from a level of coherence and clarity.

The same with your emotions. On the gross level, emotions operate like a see-saw, bringing us to opposite poles of fascination and fear, attraction and repulsion. But at the most subtle layer, emotions can flutter at powerful levels of compassion, felicity and bliss, so that your whole being reverberates in unity and love.

Your ego also can be recognized and felt as the subtle and changeable level of the mind which it really is. So instead of experiencing your ego as permanent and that which sets you apart from everyone else, you can experience it as the level of the mind where your individuality, strong concept of self, and uniqueness begin to emerge out of the wholeness of life. A subtle, but important, difference!

In short, any aspect of your existence can be the vehicle by which you reach the most subtle layer of life. Almost all self-improvement or human potential programs available today will use one or more dimensions of personality to bring you to deeper layers of your mind. For example, in our age there is an abundance of programs for the body which include diet and exercise so that your body can express its maximum potential of health and well-being. Have you ever had moments of feeling perfectly healthy and at one with your body? If so, then you know that during those moments the world seems harmonious, whole, and "alive"–the same way your body does.

On the level of your intellect, there are educational programs whose goal is to bring you to the most fundamental layer of your existence. The real aim of education is not only to teach particular subjects like math or English, but also to sharpen your mind to such a degree that it can operate on a subtle, powerful layer of universality. The greatest scientific geniuses, such as Albert Einstein and Madame Curie, have operated on this level and have uncovered scientific laws which explain the very workings of nature. In the same way, great artists have been able to reach and express very deep, subtle, and tender layers of emotion and have been able to release in us, the audience, the free and open expression of profound emotions.

So it is possible to locate transcendental consciousness at the basis of all the different dimensions of personality. And it is also possible to locate it "between" the different states of consciousness—for example, between waking and sleeping or vice-versa. This in-between state is called the "hypnogagic" state or simply "junction point."

You may have had the experience of catching yourself at the moment just before you are about to drift off to sleep. If so, you know that this is a super-charged period, often full of creative ideas. Or you may have had the experience of being "outside" yourself upon arising–not asleep, and yet not quite awake–but in a state of mind distinctly different from either one, like sitting in a theater and being a spectator to your own thoughts.

The same experience can also occur when you go directly from dreaming to waking. In the junction point, it may seem that you are not the dreamer, but the spectator who is watching the dream. At this moment, when you feel you are the spectator rather than the actor, you are experiencing the universality of transcendental consciousness.

The experience of transcendental consciousness during the juncture point is mainly unintentional. To consciously and purposefully experience transcendental consciousness you must intentionally aim at either refining the body and/or directing your attention to subtler and subtler levels of the mind. Generally speaking, it is only possible to do this while you are awake–not while you are sleeping or dreaming.

In sleep, there is simply no attention to direct. And about dreams, the psychologist Carl Jung, has pointed out, "In general, dreams are unsuitable or difficult to make use of in developing the transcendent function because they make too great demands on the subject." This means that while we are dreaming we are so caught up in the dream that we think it is reality. The demands that a dream makes upon you are so great that you give yourself completely over to the dream, and you cannot direct your attention anywhere but where the dream itself is taking you.

One final word about the aspects of personality. When we say that each level of personality has a different degree of subtlety, we need to remember that it is possible to experience both order and disorder on every level. So, for example, simply because emotion is deeper than intellect, this does not mean that anger is better than reason. Anger is emotion in disorder, while reason is intellect in order. It is possible to experience disorder and confusion both in the body and in any dimension of personality: sickness, intellectual doubt, emotional confusion, and so on.

Disorder is never desirable (although sometimes inevitable) no matter on what level, especially when it is deep. When you experience stress and disorder on a deep level, then it will disrupt the smooth functioning of other layers of your personality. For example, suppose you are clear about a friendship intellectually, but emotionally you are in turmoil. In this case, since emotions constitute a deeper layer of personality, the emotional confusion will most likely dominate and overshadow your intellectual clarity. In the opposite case, your emotional clarity would come to dominate your intellectual confusion.

Remember that stress and impurities collect on all layers of your mind, in much the same way that stress can be deposited in any part of the body. In your process of becoming whole and healthy it is only natural that you will release these stresses and impurities. Since stress is, by nature, disorder, there is no absolutely orderly way for it to be released. In the process of becoming mentally and physically normal, (especially if the process you have chosen is intense) you must inevitably display symptoms of disorder.

Also, since disorder is often deposited in deep layers of your mind, it will project itself into the surface layers–into your perceptions, feelings and actions. This is why, when you experience release of stress, you experience negative emotions such as anger or sorrow, distortion of your senses, and weak decision-making power. Obviously, when you began your search for full potential these distortions were not what you were looking for, but you need to accept the fact that they are part of the process of becoming normal. **Release of stress is certainly not the end product of growth, but it is a necessary castoff, or by-product, of growth.** To know and accept this process and to be able to handle it are, in themselves, necessary stages in your growth as an individual.

Four
Stages in the Growth of
Consciousness

One of the most successful branches of psychology is called "Developmental Psychology." This branch of psychology studies the growth of an individual in different areas of his or her life. These areas include the physical, intellectual, social, moral, financial/vocational, and ego/emotional. By studying the same individual over a long period of time as well as by studying different individuals at the same time, psychologists have discovered patterns of growth that apply to all of us. These patterns indicate that growth is a continuous process and that it proceeds in orderly stages, but of course at different rates of speed for different individuals.

The authors' own clinical experience with many people on the road to higher consciousness indicates that the same principles hold true for the growth of consciousness. Those of us on the road proceed in certain noticeable stages which we will describe in this chapter. We believe that it is vitally important for you to know what these stages are, so that you will recognize where you are and not get diverted from the path.

Remember, as we describe these stages, that development is a continuous and often overlapping process and different people proceed at different rates. For this reason, characteristics which would normally occur later could appear earlier in certain individuals–and vice-versa. Children do not skip stages in learning to walk, but they can go through certain stages, such as standing, relatively unnoticed. One day the mother will exclaim, "All of a sudden, my child started walking!" The mother never noticed the child standing, but indeed the child did. In short, some stages in the growth of consciousness will be more noticeable in some people than in others.

Before we begin our description of the stages of growth of consciousness, we need to emphasize the prior stages of growth. **You must establish yourself as a separate, independent, individuated adult before permanent stabilization in enlightenment or higher consciousness is possible.** You need to go through certain developmental stages in order to pass from childhood-adolescence to adulthood. If not, you will be stuck defending yourself from the fear of abandonment and subsequent depression associated with being on your own.

Becoming an adult involves growth in six essential areas of development. We will discuss them briefly here. We believe it is important for you to know what they are, so you will never fall into the trap of confusing the search for enlightenment with the accomplishment of adulthood.

PHYSICAL INDEPENDENCE

On the most fundamental level, this means the ability to satisfy basic physical needs such as feeding and clothing yourself. On the larger level, it is marked by responsibility for your own physical needs and behaviors as well as your ability to maintain your health, well-being, and physical development. Dependence on abusive substances such as drugs or alcohol or engaging in unsafe sexual practices is definitely not the mark of a physically responsible adult.

INTELLECTUAL INDEPENDENCE

To different degrees, adults have the ability to use logic and to reason abstractly. They can deduce what will or will not happen if they take, or do not take, certain actions. They can also draw personal, but reasonable conclusions about systems of belief. An adult mind does not readily relinquish its independence and discrimination to become an uncritical tool to be used and exploited by a group or another individual.

SOCIAL INDEPENDENCE

Developed adults are generally able to meet and get along with other people while still retaining their own individuality. They do not use membership in a group to compensate for their own inability to interact socially. Rather they are contributing members of any group they belong to, while still retaining their own individuality and their ability to interact with the community and society in general.

MORAL DEVELOPMENT

Moral adults are characterized by an inner-directed, value based sensitivity to other people and to the environment around them. Their values may be learned from parents, society, religion, or wise teachers. But once again, their values are personal and deeply felt, not the superficial and blind acting out of someone else's dictates.

VOCATIONAL/FINANCIAL RESPONSIBILITY

Able and competent adults are not regularly dependent on others for their financial resources, although they can accept help that is freely offered and does not undermine their development and independence. They do not trade their independence for someone's promises to take care of them financially.

EGO/EMOTIONAL INDEPENDENCE

Over the years in the practice of counseling and therapy and in our personal experience, we have found the most difficult transition to adulthood takes place on what we call the ego/emotional level. We use ego and emotional together because they exist at the subtlest level of the human personality, and they most often operate together. The ego is the nucleus of thoughts we have developed over time about ourselves. That ego or self-concept (thoughts individuals have about themselves) reflects what we and other people have been telling us about who we are and what we have come to believe as the truth about ourselves. Emotions are the feeling component of the personality. When we are emotionally independent, we are responsible and in charge of our own feelings—confident we can handle our own emotions, whether good or bad.

Egos that have individuated are evident in people who genuinely understand, accept, trust, and feel good about themselves as they are. However, weak egos are vulnerable egos.

They need to be constantly defended just like a weakened or wounded soldier needs to be excessively on his guard. A failure to individuate on the ego/emotional level results in defensive behaviors. These behaviors are used unconsciously to defend weakened egos. They include blaming, excuse making, attacking, avoiding, and scapegoating, to name a few. These ego defensive behaviors are associated with fear, anger, guilt and jealousy.

Separation-individuation is not complete in people who are fearful or unable to control, moderate, or even get through emotional dilemmas. Once again, because their egos are so vulnerable, they get severely upset when things don't work out the way they want. They don't believe in their own ability to get through emotional difficulties. The ego is what they have been defending all the time–a collection of thoughts they have about themselves–that ironically, they can change. Successful separation-individuation on the ego/emotional level is characterized by people with a learned confidence in their own ability to face both challenge and denial.

Let us illustrate with a case history the necessity of becoming fully adult on the ego/emotional level before enlightenment can be attained.

Lana and Carl came for counseling because of difficulties in their marriage. They both were considering divorce. Lana claimed that Carl avoided communicating with her. Carl had moved into his own apartment and claimed that Lana was continually attacking him verbally. Carl felt there was nothing about him or his behavior that was right in her eyes. When they argued, we had the distinct impression we were watching two children squabble.

Both Lana and Carl were healthy, intelligent, socially adept, financially well-off, ethical professionals. They had met ten years earlier while they were members of an internationally known consciousness expansion movement. Their growth practice consisted of extensive and intensive yoga postures, breathing exercises, meditation, special diets, advanced mental techniques, and the study of the ancient wisdom of consciousness. Both reported numerous and on-going experiences of expanded awareness, bliss, and emergence of supernormal powers. Why were two such highly evolved people, seemingly well suited for each other, unable to communicate, understand, accept, and trust each other?

During the course of counseling, it was revealed that both Lana and Carl had come from wealthy, but dysfunctional families. All their lives they had been taken care of physically and financially. They were sent to the best boarding schools and were largely protected from difficulty. What had been missing in their development was the attention, approval, affection, and acceptance necessary to become independent adults on the ego/emotional level. As such, they functioned well in their role as parents to their children, but for the most part, they were child-adolescents in their own dealings with each other. Lana was demanding, critical, and emotionally dramatic; Carl was distant, sulking, and emotionally bound-up. Neither could admit or recognize their own mistakes or characteristic flaws.

When Lana and Carl were confronted in counseling with the need to address their lack of ego/emotional maturity, they were ready to admit that the other party needed work, but largely denied their own weaknesses. To complicate matters further, they both felt their program of yoga, meditation, and other related activities would take care of all their problems. Even if they were arrested emotionally and egoically, they believed that confrontational, direct work with their ego/emotional difficulties was unnecessary.

Only after repeated encounters in counseling and repeated failures to communicate in their relationship did they begin to understand and work towards improving their interpersonal skills. Lana learned how to assert, instead of attack; Carl learned how to self-disclose, instead of avoid. Both learned to listen and cooperate more with each other. (These interpersonal skills are discussed in more detail in Chapter Five.) Only at this point were they willing to progress beyond their childish bickering and come back into harmony with each other.

Our experience in the practice of counseling and therapy confirms that many, if not most, individuals "along the path" to higher consciousness have to back up and do some work in order to become independent adults. Perhaps they have never held a steady job or earned enough money to provide for their own needs. Many have not adjusted to society outside of their own growth or spiritual group, but rather they remain child-adolescents in their interpersonal relationships.

Most growth of consciousness groups or spiritual movements assume that the people who come to them are already adults; thus, they offer little help to those who are not. This is particularly so in western culture where the tradition has been on independence and individuality. There is a tendency to disparage as unnecessary or even damaging those techniques or methods which can facilitate adult independence. Frequently the rationale for "unnecessary" is based upon the belief that the groups or movements have all that it takes to fulfill a person's needs. They contend that other techniques are damaging because they focus attention unduly on the "negative" or problem aspects of life, and this emphasis on negativity is non-life supporting.

Our response to that position is to question the basic assumption that "seekers" necessarily are adults simply because they seek a higher level of truth. Our experience confirms that this simply and frequently is just not so. Most movements that can sustain themselves over any length of time are discovering this as well. Ultimately, meditation and other related techniques result in transcendence of the ego, emotions, and even problems of life. That is not to say that from time to time we can't have transcendent experiences. We can settle down and occasionally slip past those distractions. However, the permanence or stabilization of the transcendent experience will remain elusive. Also, we transcend the ego more easily when it is strong and individuated, rather than weak.

As we said, if your ego/emotional nature is weak, you will unconsciously defend yourself through blame, attack, misplaced anger, avoidance, repression, rationalization, or any of the other defense mechanisms. **As long as there is defending, there can be no complete transcending. This is so because when we are defending our egos, we are not letting go. And letting go is necessary for transcending.** Transcendence of ego identification is necessary for enlightenment. While it is so that eastern cultures by virtue of their conditioning emphasize submission and surrender of the ego, it is also so that western cultural conditioning emphasizes the strengthening and individuation of the ego. Both are viable paths.

Imagine what would happen if someone in a weakened physical state because of hunger approached a master teacher for guidance. Most likely, the teacher would bring the seeker in and give him something to eat first. Similarly, we strongly urge seekers who need to back up and grow up to do so now.

Sharpen your interpersonal skills and face your fears of abandonment or rejection in all areas of life. This is essential. If you can't improve your interpersonal skills on your own, get help from a counselor or therapist who is experienced in working with personality disorders and interpersonal breakdowns. If the counselor or therapist knows about the growth of consciousness, then so much the better. If not, go ahead anyway. Use this book as a manual for understanding the growth of consciousness, and fill in the spaces yourself. Eventually it has to be done anyway!

Occasionally people have asked if becoming an independent adult is tantamount to becoming enlightened. We appreciate the question because it emphasizes the need to clarify carefully the subtle distinctions between the two. Becoming an independent adult means we are comfortably and solidly established in our bodies, senses, perceptions, intellects, emotions, and egos–or at least well on the way to that end.

Being enlightened means we have transcended our bodies, senses, perceptions, intellects, emotions, and egos both in and out of normal daily activity because we are established permanently in Being. Therefore, we need to become an adult before we can be enlightened. We can ultimately transcend the qualities of adulthood, but we can not by-pass these qualities.

While it is true that becoming fully adult is an immediate stepping stone to enlightenment, the two states will probably overlap from time to time along the way. But since the steps of progress can be two steps forward and one step back, the step backward may be necessary, especially when we need to back up and grow up before we can continue. Finally, while becoming an independent adult is satisfying, it is never completely fulfilling–hence: seeking.

Returning to the development of consciousness, we begin first with those stages that precede the initial experience of enlightenment. The concepts were inspired by the works of Italian psychiatrist, Roberto Assagioli, the first westerner to elucidate in some detail the special psychological characteristics that accompany the growth of consciousness. These stages are:

    I. SEEKING
    II. TEMPORARY FINDING
    III. TEMPORARY LOSING
    IV. INTENSIFICATION OF FINDING AND
         LOSING

I. SEEKING

The seeking stage is characterized by a growing sense of dissatisfaction, restlessness, meaninglessness, and seeking to put your life into a satisfying perspective. This is a natural beginning, since you cannot really begin to seek for the real truth about your life until you feel that your present situation is much too limited for you to accept. You are probably not aware of it, but what is happening at this stage is that the Self, or transcendental consciousness, is trying to emerge and is dislodging old behaviors and values. While your old behaviors are leaving, and the new experience of the Self has not yet emerged, you feel, in the words of the poet, Matthew Arnold, "Caught between two worlds/One dead, the other powerless to be born."

There is a wonderful parable which illustrates this stage:

A man was sitting on the bank of a river looking across the river to the other bank. He felt, without knowing exactly why, that life would be better for him on the other shore. So he got in a boat and proceeded to row across the river. But when he got to the middle of the river, fog set in and the water became very choppy. He thought maybe it was better to go back where he came from. But looking around, he realized it would be just as difficult to go back again as it would to go forward. By this time, the fog was very thick so he just rowed blindly, hoping against hope to reach his destination. Finally he arrived at the other shore, and being very tired, he lay down and took a rest. When he awoke, he enjoyed his beautiful surroundings and was happy that he had made the trip. He looked across the river to see the shore where he had come from but was startled to find that there was no shore, nor was there a river or a boat. The destination he had come to was real enough, but it was as if everything before that, including the journey itself, was a dream or an illusion.

The journey is like the seeking stage. You are dissatisfied with your present position, but unable to have a firm grasp on what you really want. To leave the old for the new, you need to go through a period of uncertainty, which may seem dangerous and frightening, but which is unavoidable. When you reach your goal, it almost seems as if you never really went anywhere, because what you are looking for is already inside you. It was simply your own unbounded potential.

The seeking stage can occur virtually at any time in our lives, from adolescence to old age. In middle age it might be called a mid-life crisis, but the same symptoms often appear during adolescence when young people express dissatisfaction with life as they experience it but are unable to come up with a clear and better alternative. Because the alternative is not clear (if it were, there would be no necessity for seeking!), our activity in the seeking stage is characterized by a kind of aimless and random restlessness.

Just as the seeking stage can occur at any time during our lives, it can also last for any length of time. Sometimes it may last for years, even a lifetime. Sometimes it will be so short as to be hardly noticed. Often, it is a time of moral and religious crisis when you seriously question former beliefs and standards of right and wrong. This stage is very disturbing and nagging, but it has its own built-in remedy—as the pain of meaninglessness grows, so does your urge to do something about it.

In fact, the most important value of the seeking stage is that it is the motivator of later growth. Once you catch the first glimpses of the idea that there is more to life than the boundaries you are living in, then your true Self can no longer be kept hidden. And the emerging energy of your true Self will uproot whatever is in its way. This uprooting is the same purification that we discussed under the mechanics of stress release.

At this point, the Self, or transcendental consciousness, is only at best a glimpse, not at all a clear experience. The pain that we experience at this stage is an indication that something wrong is going right, (unstressing) and we are moving on to another level of life. At this stage many people look for and find guidance from a source which claims to know the fundamental meaning of life. Religion, philosophy, psychotherapy, and many self-improvement programs, represent some of these sources.

Sometimes the search ends here and sometimes you must go from one source to another until you find a truly satisfactory or comfortable alternative to the suffering and discomfort which you are experiencing. Without a satisfactory alternative, life will go on as an aimless struggle. But remember, seeking is a necessary preparation for the journey to complete development, and it has always been this way. Thousands of years ago the Greek philosopher, Aristotle, stated, "All knowledge begins in wonder."

A case history here can help clarify the seeking stage in the development of consciousness. Roger, a thirty-five year old building contractor, came to therapy with a variety of symptoms, including impulsive sex and eating behaviors, mood swings, a history of unstable relationships, identity disturbance, fears of abandonment by others, and chronic feelings of boredom. All of these were symptoms of what is called the "borderline personality disorder." Several years earlier, Roger had stopped his impulsive drinking and drug abuse (also borderline symptoms), and now was committed to making additional progress in his life. What placed his case within the realm of psychological disturbances accompanying the growth of consciousness was his portrayal of how he was somehow "outside himself" or witnessing much of his own confusion and doubt at this time.

Roger wasn't sure what exactly he was looking for in therapy. To the statement: "Do you feel you can't go forward, can't go backwards, nor can you stay where you are?", Roger excitedly said, "That's it exactly!" Further questioning and clarification confirmed for Roger that what he really wanted to know was what life was about at its deepest level. He was "seeking."

Roger had never been involved in any consciousness raising activities, nor had he done any reading in this area. At the end of the first session, Roger was given a draft of this book and encouraged to search deeply within himself for verification as he read carefully. Roger returned the next week visibly uplifted. Roger was able to fill a gap in his own intellectual understanding about his experiences, and use his new-found understanding of the Self or awareness as a basis for his therapy, which now progressed at an accelerated pace.

Not only was Roger able to defuse his impulses, reduce his attack and avoidance behaviors, catch himself when he engaged in irrational thinking, but also he broadened his experience of the silent witness through breathing and meditation techniques, which he learned quickly and easily. Roger, an earnest seeker, began to realize that his former impulsive and often self-destructive behaviors were motivated by a sincere desire for inner peace and happiness. He began to experience and discover in his own life what he was actually looking for.

II. TEMPORARY FINDING

The stage which we call temporary finding is a giant step on the road to enlightenment. It is the first clear experience we have of transcendental consciousness or the Self. In religious terms, it is a feeling of great spiritual insight and discovery. In psychological terms, it is a newly found self-discovery, a feeling of freedom from old bonds.

In this stage your true Self bursts through to the surface in the same way that a seed (which has been lying dormant in the ground) suddenly sprouts. All of a sudden, (or it seems that way) the Self bursts through the shell of ignorance and stress, and the experience is exhilarating–charged with energy, light, profound meaning, and wholeness. After this experience, you feel that you will never be the same again.

Some people have this experience after long years of searching. But other people have this experience who would never have thought of themselves as seekers. If you are in this second group and you think back on your life before your profound experience, you will surely find that, in fact, you were a seeker and even had most of the experiences of seeking, even though you were never consciously aware of it.

The intensity of the first experience of the Self will naturally vary from individual to individual. Sometimes it can be very gentle and sometimes so overpowering that it seems more than you can handle. But the value for you of this experience has little to do with the intensity—as long as it is a clear experience. The real value has to do with how you integrate this experience into your life as a daily living activity. And, in turn, this integration depends on your basic physical, psychological, and spiritual health.

The authors assume that there are a few individuals whose first experience of the Self is integrated into their lives with little or no disturbance. But our practice tells us that these individuals are the rare exceptions. Less exceptional, but still rare, are those individuals whose disturbance is only on the intellectual level. For those individuals a simple explanation of their experience is enough to remove their confusion.

For the great majority of us, however, the first experience of our deepest Self releases huge blocks of stress, and this is accompanied by a charge of pent-up emotions which is powerful and often uncontrollable. What is exposed is an ego that is much in need of attention, approval, affection, and acceptance. In this stage you could have frequent emotional outbursts that are easily provoked.

Sometimes your emotions will flare up with no provocation at all. You find yourself easily excitable, suddenly elated and overly enthusiastic. Sometimes these emotions are accompanied by sobbing and floods of tears. The experiences here are like those of a person who reacts to instant and surprising success, such as winning a large amount of money or receiving news that a loved one feared dead or lost is actually alive and safe. These experiences are generally positive but also quite rough and uncontrollable.

Deeper even than the emotional disturbance of this stage is confusion on the level of your ego. What may be exposed is an ego much in need of attention, approval, and affection. Without a proper perspective at this time, either from your own knowledge or from a good teacher, it is all too easy to identify the newly found Self with your own needy ego, which will result in a falsely inflated ego and an unrealistic notion of who and what you really are.

It is understandably tempting to confine the expanding sense of energy and awareness to your own small boundaries. When this happens, however, the unlimited experience of "Greatness" itself becomes lost or forgotten, and what remains is the limited experience of "I am great.'

When taken together, the experience of "Greatness" and the feeling, "I am great" are certainly both valid experiences. But if you are so confused as to completely forget the former, then you may begin to believe that you are the greatness, rather than just the expression of the greatness. This is foolish, and in extreme cases, even dangerous. Tyranny, fanaticism, and delusions of power all have their roots in this confusion.

Another general area of confusion in this stage occurs because we naturally attribute an aura of greatness to the method, teachings, teacher, or whatever means may have helped us to achieve our first clear experience of the Self. Now, it is only natural to feel a very deep sense of gratitude to whatever or whoever helped us along the path, and even to feel a sense of indebtedness which we want to repay through our service to a group or teacher. But such gratitude and service sometimes become so concentrated as to exclude everything else in our environment–social concerns, family concerns, concerns for our own health and concern to always have an open mind. Again, in extreme cases, this leads to inflexible and ruthless behavior which we see today in some otherwise well-intentioned cult members.

An example of ego inflation can be seen in the case of Paul, a thirty-four year old health professional. When Paul came for help, his life was falling apart around him. Despite the chaos in his domestic and professional life, he still maintained a naive and somewhat arrogant attitude about how best to address his difficulties. Paul's many years of association with a consciousness-expansion movement had opened him to numerous experiences of the transcendent and provided him with profound intellectual understanding of the process. His understanding and the experience of "basking in the bliss," as he called it, imbued him with tremendous gratitude and reverence for the movement he was associated with and for its founder and leader.

Paul was a zealous advocate for his movement, and his behavior was very sanctimonious. He brashly preached, heatedly argued, and even demanded acceptance of his positions from any and all. Consequently he alienated himself from his parents and siblings; provoked disdain from his colleagues, to the extent that he even lost his last two jobs; and uprooted his wife and family several times, resulting in domestic turmoil, in order to get closer to "the teaching." Even with all the difficulties that ensued physically, mentally, financially, and socially, Paul relentlessly insisted this was what he had to go through to reach enlightenment.

In Paul's quest for spiritual perfection or realization of the Self, he had exposed an ego or self concept that appeared inflated on the surface, but was really weak. Paul badly needed the acceptance, affection, attention, and approval he had not received as a boy–something he simply could not admit to himself, because he believed he was "way above this sort of weakness."

In fact, although Paul's inner experiences of bliss were authentic and personally valuable, he had used these experiences to mask an ego that was much in need of attention, affection and approval. Indeed, he had used a stage in his growth–"Finding"–to stunt further growth. Only through extensive counseling was Paul able to trust his therapist, who helped him break down the narcissistic defenses of his ego. Subsequently, he was able to reflect on how defensive he had been and how those defenses were affecting those around him. Slowly Paul was able to temper his behavior with more effective interpersonal skills. Paul had begun to "get out of his head" and get more "into his heart."

In all of these cases of finding, our nervous systems are unable to fully and readily integrate the transcendental experience, and what comes to dominate temporarily is a confusion of intellect, emotions, and ego. In the same way that a photo flash dazzles your eyes for a time and leaves you unable to focus, so does the previously unexperienced light of the Self dazzle the different dimensions of your personality.

III. TEMPORARY LOSING

In time, the intensity of your initial experience as well as the accompanying confusion seem to just fizzle out. This will be true no matter how positive or how intense was your first experience of the Self. Of course this is disappointing, but there are very positive reasons why this happens. The primary reason is simply that our nervous systems need to adjust to and integrate this experience. You might say that this is nature's way of infusing the experience of the transcendent or Self into all aspects of our personality and physiology.

A fully developed individual is one who is permeated with Self on all levels of his or her existence. Therefore, the fact that you have an initial "flashy" experience is indication that there is a real gap between your ordinary self and your deepest true Self. Your ultimate goal is to bridge this gap and integrate your daily life with transcendental consciousness. In this way transcendental consciousness becomes an integral aspect of your daily life.

Another factor in this stage of temporary losing is the contrast effect. Our first experience of anything unusual obviously has a much greater effect when contrasted with our later experience of the same thing. When we try to recapture the effect of the first experience we are hardly ever successful. These later attempts to recapture the first experience of the transcendent appear to lack excitement, and so we find ourselves in the stage which we have called temporary losing.

Because the experience of finding was so emotionally uplifting, the inevitable stage of temporary losing will lead to discouragement. Try in whatever way you can, nothing quite so powerful and exhilarating as the initial experience or experiences seem to be happening. After a while you get to the point of actually questioning and even doubting the reality of your initial experience. "Was it just an illusion?" "Did I bring it on myself through imagination by wanting it so much?" "Was it a dream?" "An emotional high that didn't mean as much as I thought it did?"

Frequently this questioning mounts and turns into bitterness and cynicism. Before, you were espousing lofty ideals to others, ideals which you believed in without a shadow of a doubt. Now you aren't so sure. You even begin to feel tinges of resentment towards your beliefs, knowledge, teacher, and the principles which you thought would always guide you through your life.

At this point it is very common to try to return to your former set of beliefs, habits, allegiances and so forth. This particular point of the journey is similar to the point in the parable we told at the beginning of this chapter—where the seeker is caught in the middle of the river, with no sight of either his destination or the place he started from.

The fact is that whether we are two weeks into our journey or two years, we are simply unable to return to our former ways of doing and thinking. Once you have experienced even a glimpse of the radiance of your true Self, nothing else can substitute. Of course, people try to go backwards and sometimes even force themselves to return to former lifestyles. But there is not much likelihood that this can bring long-term satisfaction.

This frustrating state of affairs—not being able to go backwards or forwards—leads to anger. Essentially, anger is the inability to satisfy one's desires or goals, and this is exactly where we are at this stage. You want repeatedly clear experiences of the transcendent, but you cannot attain them.

After you repeatedly and unsuccessfully try to reach this goal, eventually the attitude of "nothing I do makes any difference" takes hold. What may set in is a phenomenon known in behavioral psychology as "learned helplessness." The strength of the ego dissipates, self-esteem is deflated and helplessness, indecision and the loss of will-power appear to dominate. You get the feeling that you are hopelessly stuck.

Sheila, an attractive forty-two year old secretary came for therapy because of just such a sense of losing. She had begun the practice of meditation several years ago and claimed it had, at the time, transformed her life. Prior to starting meditation, Sheila freely indulged in what she called "the million dollar hits" in life. These "hits" included sex, food, drugs, and alcohol, all of which she became disenchanted with in time. Sheila became a seeker.

Meditation temporarily satisfied Sheila's desire for esoteric experiences, and the intellectual theory which accompanied her meditative practice inspired her. For Sheila, it was as if she had found the ultimate "million dollar hit." Unfortunately (or in actuality, fortunately), Sheila's experiences in meditation were short lived. When, in her words, meditation became "dry as a potato chip in the desert," she became discouraged. In a rush of desperation, she backed up and renewed her restless seeking.

You name it, and Sheila tried it: crystal gazing and healing, exotic herbal remedies, fortune telling, tarot cards, other forms of meditation, mediums, long retreats, and body work of all types. But nothing seemed to work. There were no more flashy experiences. Bitterness and cynicism set in, and an angry and disappointed Sheila voiced resentment that she "had been had" by the oldest con game in history. At this point, she lapsed further into a state of helplessness and depression.

When Sheila began her therapy, she was most helped by a clear understanding of the stages commonly experienced during the growth of consciousness. She began to appreciate that a long history of attachment to excitement and emotional "highs" had been transferred into a rather unrealistic expectation of enlightenment. In effect, enlightenment for her was experienced as another unsatisfying emotional high.

The rush of unstressing that Sheila experienced merely reinforced this thinking. At the same time, an ego or self-concept which had been long in need of attention was exposed–

hence the doubt and discouragement when the flashy experiences faded. In this regard, affirmations of her self worth and life as it is, versus life as she thought it should be, were helpful.

We are reminded here of the story of a contemporary student who was relating an experience to his spiritual teacher. This experience was simply one of silent awareness which was present all the time, even when sleeping. The student commented how life went on just as it had before–nothing dramatic. There was still pleasure and pain, joy and sadness. He told his teacher that if this was enlightenment, there wasn't much to it. The teacher responded, "That's right; there is not much to it."

IV. INTENSIFICATION OF FINDING AND LOSING

Now it is nature to the rescue. Many living things seem to have a period of incubation where nothing seems to be happening on the surface. There is calm before the storm. The stage of temporary losing inevitably weakens its grip on us and the next stage enters, which we have labeled, "intensification of finding and losing."

Because of the difference in each person's nervous system, it is impossible to predict exactly where this stage will take over from the stage of temporary losing. However, the very knowledge of the stages which we have been discussing will definitely ease the passage from one to the other. This is especially true of the transition between temporary losing and intensification of finding and losing. If you have a clear understanding of what is happening during temporary losing, you will not be frightened or become desperate or try in vain to revert to your old lifestyle.

The main reason for the occurrence of the intensification stage has to do with the mechanics of stress release which we discussed in the earlier chapters. Even though it was followed by a loss, temporary finding made a significant breakthrough in the armour of stress. This release of stress was followed by a new-found sense of freedom and energy. Your nervous system integrates this experience, stabilizes itself without any apparent forward movement and then prepares for further growth. This initial breakthrough has prepared or loosened the nervous system to experience more breakthroughs followed by more periods of integration and stability, (temporary losing). Thus the stage labeled, "intensification of finding and losing."

The rapid alternation of finding and losing the Self has dramatic effects on the physiology and personality because it is accompanied by the rapid release of stress. Senses which were previously blocked or distorted by stress are now freed, and sight, sounds, smells, and touches become enlivened and extremely sensitive. In this stage also, many people become sensitive, often overly so, to their immediate surroundings and to their environment in general. Personal conflicts which you witnessed or took part in now become extremely irritating, and you go out of your way to avoid these and other aggravating situations. You become more discriminating in your choice of friends and, in general, more sharply discriminating about anything likely to affect your mind and body—the foods you eat, the television shows you watch, and the ecology around you.

The rapid unstressing which is going on during this stage sometimes creates rather bizarre scenarios which may be easily taken for delusions or psychotic hallucinations. The emerging awareness in the individual that he or she is "watching" these experiences as they are taking place clearly marks the difference between the growth of consciousness and psychosis.

It is worth repeating at this point that the psychotic is retreating from reality or awareness and the seeker is increasingly in touch with reality.

Your emotions, always a sensitive part of the personality, are especially affected during this stage. Rapid mood swings, ups and downs, heaven and hell, often follow on the heels of each other. Partly because you are so caught up in these emotional swings, the practical affairs of day-to-day life seem complex and demanding. When this state of affairs becomes noticeable to your friends and family, they naturally become concerned, suspicious, and often attempt to discourage you. This discouragement results in even more emotional upheaval.

During this stage, rapid adjustments will also occur on the level of the ego or personal identity. With the growth of consciousness, comes the growing awareness that "I" am not limited or bound by those aspects of my personality which I formerly thought to be me, but am infinitely greater. Simultaneously, though, comes another sort of awareness which is bound to be disturbing—that is the discovery that even those aspects of my personality which I thought were permanent have, in fact, changed. You can wonder at this stage who you really are.

A new and more natural personality is emerging, but you may be very disturbed by the loss of what you always thought was your real identity. The face or "mask" you have been wearing loosens and melts away to reveal a new and different you. While the process may be disturbing, the end result is always favorable. Neurotics, who are well known for their inability to relax facial muscles, find relief coupled with a sense of strangeness about what they see in the mirror.

All in all, this last stage is the most precarious one to live through. In certain past societies which were organized along religious and spiritual lines, monasteries or ashrams often supported the individual through this stage. In such a supportive environment the passage through this particular stage of the individual's growth could be nurtured and supported in the most delicate manner.

In our own contemporary society we have few facilities to attend to this condition. Contemporary hospitals provide little or no help and in most cases would simply worsen the situation. Most of what can be done today must be done by the person himself with the support of family and friends and perhaps those helping professionals who are understanding enough to support the natural unfolding process. Little, outside of understanding, support, and a few natural procedures, (suggested in Chapter Five) are required. If left to be, the unfolding is an automatic process.

Mike was a thirty-eight year old businessman who taught oriental martial arts in his spare time. He consulted us because "all kinds of things were happening," and he thought he could be "losing it." More specifically, Mike was disturbed by feelings that he was floating in the air over his body while he was sleeping, that people were looking at him as a very strange person, that his family was increasingly criticizing him, and that his friends were frequently arguing with him about his life style. For Mike, the mornings were the worst part of the day. He woke up anxious and unable to settle down. His inability to relax usually led to his being down on himself for not being able to do so. By the afternoon and evening, Mike was relaxed, buoyant, and confident. Everyday his life was like hell, then heaven.

During the 1960s, Mike had adopted the "hippie" lifestyle and appearance and spent a year in India seeking the truth about life. There he had had a breakthrough, and in his words "things finally fell into place." When he returned to the states, he got a haircut and went "straight," feeling this was definitely the way for him to go. He took over the family business, but years later blamed this course of action for "lulling him into the sleep" of money and materialism.

After a period of depression, Mike renewed with vigor his spiritual practices and managed to break through again. Mike again changed his outward appearance by growing a beard, letting his hair grow long, radically altering his diet, and quitting the bar scene where he had met with business buddies.

As a result of these changes, Mike couldn't find anyone who understood or accepted him. He felt isolated and became suspicious and mistrustful of others. Looking in a mirror was the most disturbing experience for Mike, because he wasn't at all sure who was looking back.

At this point Mike needed to stabilize his growth, rather than accelerate it by using new techniques. In fact, he was encouraged to cut back his daily program of movement centering, meditation, and strict dieting for a while. Understanding, reinforcement, and keeping a vision of the goal while he passed through this tumultuous stage helped Mike considerably. He broke off with his drinking buddies, moved to the country, made new acquaintances with some supportive people in an eclectic "new age" church. Eventually, he settled back into the family business, but at a much less intense pace. His parents came to accept him as a different but now a more responsible and happy person.

———————◇———————

Now you should have a clear understanding of the four stages in the growth of consciousness before the enlightenment experience is stabilized. Now you also know some specific, important characteristics of each of these stages. So that you can have a complete grasp of this process, we will comment in more detail on some of the characteristics which are common to all of these stages. Remember, any symptom could occur at any time or stage because of the individual differences in the development process. Three symptoms, however, frequently cut across the boundaries of all stages.

The first common characteristic is what we have called "intellectual confusion." Your intellect is your ability to understand, apply, analyze, synthesize, and judge. It is always eager to process any event or experience. Your intellect is naturally drawn to new, different, or strange experiences and will not rest until such experiences have been understood. The rapid changes that occur during the growth of consciousness can be the source of this disturbance of intellect. Therefore, it is necessary as much as possible to always keep near the forefront of your mind what is happening to you. Intellectual understanding is your security blanket through this whole process. Having it is not the ultimate solution, but not having it during this process can make your life seem intolerable.

Another common characteristic is social rejection. Most of us are social animals and are seldom alone for long periods of time. We have a natural affinity for other people's company, and especially when we are going through a crisis, we need their understanding, support and acceptance.

But the rapid changes in thought, speech and action and the whole array of new behavior that we act out during this stage of growing consciousness sometimes leads to rejection by people on whom we are used to relying. This rejection is an indirect result of the changes you are going through. Parents, friends, spouses and co-workers are accustomed to thinking of you in a set pattern. When your behavior changes from that set pattern, they become disturbed. Either because they fail to understand the reasons for your changes or because their attitude toward you is very inflexible, they tend to reject you, rather than change the way they look at you.

This rejection often takes the form of ridicule, or termination of the relationship. The results are not only unpleasant, but sometimes temporarily disruptive of your growth. These negative results can often be avoided or lessened with effective communication strategies which we will give you in the next chapter.

Last of the characteristics or symptoms that are common to all the stages is one which we call, "witnessing" or out-of-body experience. Witnessing, like all the other characteristics we have been discussing, is not at all a sign of mental illness. In fact it is the consequence and particularly positive indication of the growth of consciousness. R. D. Laing, the British psychiatrist, described this condition very accurately: "There is a persistent scission [division] between the Self and the body. What the individual regards as his true self is experienced as more or less disembodied, and bodily experiences are in turn felt to be part of the false-self system."

Similar experiences are frequently reported to the authors by individuals undergoing the rapid growth of consciousness. We hear such statements as, "I looked down at my morning bowl of cereal and felt that I was completely outside of myself. I started eating but it didn't really seem like my hand bringing the cereal up to my mouth because I was watching the whole process."

At first this experience is very strange indeed, even alarming. Some people may wonder if they are losing their minds. But there is a very reasonable explanation for this experience based on the process we have outlined for the growth of consciousness. The essential reasons for the seeming out-of-body experience is that the Self was heretofore experienced only in brief and quiet moments of little or no activity. Now, the Self is beginning to show itself in activity. The first few times it happens, it seems very strange. As with other experiences, the contrast effect is operating here and the novelty will diminish with repeated exposure.

It would appear that the inability to distinguish between the self and the Self may lead to the conclusion that there is a basic division in who we really are. This conclusion is false and will not arise if you have the proper understanding and guidance. Every person is multi-faceted, with different aspects of personality (the self) and an essential Self which remains constant (though sometimes hidden) throughout his or her life. When the Self begins to emerge, some people get very confused and feel they are becoming "split personalities."

A sudden and unexpected experience of transcendental consciousness in daily activity may indeed temporarily disorient your perceptions. This is particularly true in people who do not have a strong sense of their own ego or personal identity. These people may have spent a lot of time and energy in their lives trying to discover their individual identity. When a different and unknown phase of themselves (the Self) begins to enter their daily activity, this has the temporary effect of even further disorganizing these attempts.

Well-intentioned psychologists and other helping professionals without the right understanding of the difference between the self and the Self could easily make a bad situation worse. For one thing, they could be all too ready to slap labels such as "schizophrenia" or "psychosis" on this experience of witnessing. Therefore, it is important for us to emphasize and reiterate that witnessing is a sign of growing health and fullness. Even when witnessing seems very disturbing to you, it has positive conditions that are never present in psychosis. These positive conditions include an awareness of the disturbing experience while it occurs, absence of total immersion in the disturbance and recognizing that one is in fact confused or disoriented.

As the inner silent Self becomes more predominant, stabilized, and integrated, you will be increasingly able to sustain the experience of witnessing in daily activity. You will find that witnessing is in fact a liberating and exhilarating experience. Your true Self is now assuming its rightful and natural place in your life. You begin to realize that you are not the limited, personal identity or the "I" you previously thought you were, but are the infinitely greater, unbounded field of pure awareness or Self, the silent witness to all activity.

It is the experience of the authors that, given the proper understanding and support, the dilemma posed by witnessing is readily overcome. Of course, the experience of witnessing will not cease after the confusion abates, but it will become enjoyable. Fortunately, many self-improvement programs take special care to ground their students in the intellectual distinction between self and Self (although the terms may differ from group to group). With assurance and support, this critical period will end. If it does happen, however, that you feel a basic weakness in your personality has become exposed, then you may want to seek professional counseling. This would be the exception.

The experience of the transcendent, although it has occasional outbursts, is most often a gradual and progressive one, and its effects are positive and growth oriented. Therefore, its ultimate effect will be to bring out the best in you. Also, with the emergence in the world of so many groups dedicated to higher consciousness, isolated cases of severe confusion should become fewer and support systems of sympathy and understanding greater.

Since this book concerns itself with psychological disturbances accompanying the growth of consciousness, we have not referred very much to the more advantageous, satisfying and uplifting characteristics of that same growth. But of course, ultimately speaking, what is most important about the growth of consciousness is the experience of enlightenment itself or the growth of full potential.

We can begin our brief description of the healthy human being with some of the characteristics of the "self-actualized" person described by the great psychologist, Abraham Maslow.

1. Clearer, more efficient perception of reality.
2. More openness to experience.
3. Increased integration, wholeness and unity of the person.
4. Increased spontaneity, expressiveness, full functioning, aliveness.
5. A real self, (ego) a firm identity, autonomy, aliveness.
6. Increased objectivity, detachment, transcendence of self (ego).
7. Recovery of creativeness.
8. Ability to fuse concreteness and abstractness.
9. Democratic character structure.
10. Ability to love.

To the authors, these represent a fairly complete list of the characteristics we have found developing in people going through a transformation of consciousness. These are the psychological rewards of the growth of consciousness. They are the reasons, we might say, why we are willing to undergo the disturbances that accompany this growth.

Without these positive signs or rewards, the disturbances would not be the means to an end but only the symptoms of inner psychological weakness. When the positive signs of the growth of consciousness appear more frequently, then this is an indication of a more rapid transition from the disturbing side effects to enlightenment. You may continue to experience disturbances temporarily, but the progress of your evolution will continue and will even accelerate.

The measurable characteristics of the healthy human specimen listed above do not constitute a permanent state free from problems. Maslow pointed this out when he commented on his own concept of self-actualization. "Our aim," he states, "is to correct the widespread misunderstanding of self-actualization as a static, unreal 'perfect' state in which all human problems are transcended. To make the fact clearer, I could describe self-actualization as a development of personality which frees the person from the deficiency problems of growth."

Self-actualization, then, is more of a process than a permanent state. Maslow's points are a description of the positive characteristics accompanying the growth of consciousness. The permanent state of enlightenment has been called by many names and described in many ways. One name which we think is very apt and fits in with the process of growth described in this book is "self-realization."

Self-realization means simply that your deepest Self, hitherto just a hidden potential, is now a living reality in your daily life, or in other words, has been made real. A simple and eloquent description of the permanent state of enlightenment or self-realization is given by the philosopher and teacher Maharishi Mahesh Yogi. For our purposes we can summarize this description as follows:

1. Permanent
On the way to the state of enlightenment, transcendental consciousness has been repeatedly experienced and blocks of stress have been progressively released. When the last deep rooted stress is released, then the Self comes out to stay. It is as if the last cloud of stress has vanished and the sun is now out in all its glory. Your mind and body have been conditioned to experience alternating states of inner awareness (Self) and activity, until it actually feels normal to experience the Self in activity. The more you experience the Self in activity, the more stress you dissolve and, in turn, the more stress you dissolve, the more clearly you will be able to experience the Self. Certain long-term stresses may continue, but their intensity will be small and they will not interfere with or overshadow the Self. Eventually, the realization that "I am the unbounded Self" becomes permanent.

2. A Natural or Normal State
We use the words "natural" or "normal" interchangeably. In the beginning stages of the enlightenment experience, virtually all of the deep rooted stresses have been released and the mind and body can function in a truly natural state. You come to realize that the stresses you have been living with are really an unnatural burden on your life, like a sickness or sore which

interferes with your normal functioning. The "normal" for you becomes not the average, but the natural and effortless, since absence of effort is the hallmark of natural. This effortlessness is the "freedom to be" on the most profound level. This freedom includes freedom from problems, which instead become situations to be met and dealt with in an easy and comfortable manner and not situations to be identified with or over-shadowed by.

3. Actions Are Supported By Nature
Nature supports itself. When you are free from the unnatural influence of stress and you are living the Self you will automatically act in a natural manner. The Self is your link to the universe and to the fundamental and eternal laws of nature. When you have established that link, then the will or purpose of nature becomes your own will or purpose. Everything you do fits into the natural scheme of the universe and you have the feeling of "all being well and wisely put." Even events in your life which appear negative or destructive are seen as being part of the continual process of growth and expansion which you are a part of. You come to realize that the swings of the pendulum of life are parts of one process. Your own actions in relation to those around you and to the environment as a whole become life-supporting.

4. Living 200% of Your Life
This means that now the inner silent value of life, pure awareness, or the Self, is established along with the outer active value of life. Both are necessary in order to live a full life. In answer to the question of whether life is essentially an eternal and unchanging absolute field, or relative and always changing, you can answer it is both. Firmly established in the

non-changing Self, you can live your day-to-day life in the active world with complete enjoyment and fulfillment. This equals 200% of life. When these four values are added to Maslow's characteristics of a self-actualized person, we get a clear picture of what we mean by enlightenment. Of course, there are numerous other descriptions for the enlightenment experience, depending on the angle that a particular teaching or path has about this goal. Ultimately though, all teachings and paths describe a oneness between the individual and the universe.

————◇————

Development is a continuous process and it proceeds to stages even beyond the ones we have described. Further refinement of the mind and body allow all dimensions of your life to reach their fullest capacity. The senses become attuned to very fine levels, not available on the grosser level and become extra-sensory. Supernormal powers such as knowledge of future events, subtle communication with others at a distance, speaking in foreign or strange languages, and the ability to heal others have been reported and can arise.

Experience reaches a celestial level that was previously just esoteric speculation but is now perceived as real. The intellect blossoms and becomes capable of discriminating and cognizing at the most subtle levels. And at these levels, the universe reveals its most profound secrets. The emotions explode with love, which is ignited by devotion to the knowledge, teaching, or teacher that has made your growth possible. Your own individual ego is now perceived as a manifestation of the infinite and eternal flame.

The gap closes between inner and outer, subject and object. All that was once thought to be finite and bounded is now experienced as infinite and unbounded. At this summit in the growth of consciousness, harmony and unity prevail within the individual and radiate outwards to become a positive and supportive influence for family, friends, society, and environment.

Five
Natural Therapeutic Techniques

In this chapter, we will present to you a number of measures you can apply to help ease the transition in your growth toward higher consciousness. Our purpose in saving these for the last chapter has not been to keep you in suspense or to save the best for the last; we wanted you to acquire a clear understanding of the mechanics of stress release as well as the stages in the growth of consciousness. Without this understanding, you would not be motivated to apply these techniques or know when and how to apply them. Remember also, that your understanding will grow as your experience deepens, and it will benefit you to refer back to this book periodically.

The techniques which we will now recommend to you are based on two main points of understanding. The first point is one which we have emphasized throughout this book and is the chief factor which distinguishes disturbances in the growth of consciousness from psychosis or mental illness. It is that the individual in transition is "standing outside," witnessing the disturbance as it occurs, and is fully aware that something is wrong. Sometimes the individual is so aware that the very mental mechanics leading up to or causing the disturbance are observed while they are happening.

The second point of understanding also has been implicit throughout this book. Even though we cannot and should not ignore these disturbances, our ultimate concern is for the growth and not for the disturbances. At any point in the growth toward higher consciousness, including those periods when you are experiencing disturbances, you should be able to easily make a list of the gains you have made in the recent past. You know, therefore, that the disturbances are signs of your growth.

These two points of understanding form the basis for a helpful approach that does not interfere with the instinctive tendencies of the body and mind to purify and heal themselves. Any therapy which tries forcefully to break down your ego defenses or probe your unconscious is generally out of place here. Such a therapy would proceed from the mistaken idea that you are trying to block something deep inside you and are building all sorts of defenses in order to do this. But in your case, the disturbances are not signs of blocking but rather of unblocking (release of stress).

So any further vigorous attempts to remove blocks would just artificially interfere with a natural process **already** underway. This does not mean that insight, or understanding your own defenses is unhealthy, but more the spontaneous by-product of growth. As one expands in consciousness, the unconscious reveals itself. Good therapists will facilitate this process without control or force.

The measures which we suggest to you have as their goal simply to facilitate, integrate and stabilize the gains which you are making or have already made. They may be applied by yourself to yourself; or by yourself to others as you help them through difficult stages; or they can be used as a set of standards by which you evaluate the relevance and usefulness of any therapy you are receiving. Even though these techniques can be self-applied, we will frequently address you as if you were a counselor helping others. This may help you to be more objective about helping others, as well as yourself.

As with most forms of therapy, the first step is to listen carefully to and observe the symptoms. Prying and probing will not be of much value. Remember that intense probing or other powerful confrontational techniques to uncover the unconscious can be potentially damaging. Through the mechanics of stress release, the natural process of bringing to the surface what is supposed to come out is already underway. At most, some encouragement to speak freely is all that is necessary.

The person who is discussing his or her symptoms will experience the usual relief that comes with open discussion. That relief may be particularly lacking in some cases because many seekers of higher consciousness belong to groups, or subscribe to beliefs, which encourage only positive thinking. They have been taught that the universe is purposeful and meaningful and that they have a positive role to play. Therefore, when they hit a low spot in their lives, they feel that they are being unfaithful to their teaching and are embarrassed to discuss it. However, once a person feels empathy and non-judgmental acceptance from the person he or she is talking to, then a big weight is lifted and the discussion can flow freely. With this, we have the proper environment for the presentation of nine specific techniques which follow.

INTELLECTUAL UNDERSTANDING

We have discussed this throughout the book and we include it here for further explanation and to remind you that it is not just comfortable to have an explanation, but is absolutely necessary. We have noticed that people who come to us suffering from the heavy release of stress often have one set of complaints which overrides all others. That is the air of confusion, disbelief or mystery surrounding their situation. As soon as they receive some explanation, the air begins to clear.

In the case of people who are releasing stress, it seems to be an immense relief to understand the cause of their symptoms. The sequence of events which led to their present predicament seems logical when properly understood and provides a reasonable basis for future action. Without proper understanding, we live in needless fear. It is like groping in a dark cave listening to mysterious and frightening sounds. Once a light is brought in, we know where we are. We can see the trickle of water over the rocks and the small, chirping birds who have made their nest in the cave.

With the light on, our fears disappear. This is the benefit of intellectual understanding. As soon as we have it, we begin to release the emotion of fear and are ready to take the next step. Without it, we live in constant fear–fear of the unknown, fear of being a helpless victim and fear of losing our minds due to uncontrollable impulses.

An example of this was the case of Ralph, a twenty-six year old laborer. We saw him just after he had been hospitalized for a few days for what was diagnosed as a "brief reactive psychosis." Ralph was a strong but sensitive person and had overextended himself at home and at work to the point of exhaustion. His physical exhaustion was paralleled by a breakdown and disorganization of thoughts and behavior. With a few days of rest, Ralph was back to his old self and released from the hospital.

However, both he and his wife were very confused about this event, and they lived in fear of its recurring. When he presented his symptoms to us, we saw that he was extremely perceptive and intuitive, sometimes anticipating almost exactly what we were going to say. This gave us the clue that perhaps we were dealing with a person whose consciousness was growing, even though he had experienced a recent bout of turmoil.

While we were discussing his symptoms in more detail, Ralph revealed that he frequently felt "outside" himself, and was a neutral observer of his own thoughts and actions. In fact, he knew that his behavior during his breakdown was bizarre while it was occurring, but he also felt that he needed help; and so he "watched" himself being carried into the ambulance. During the entire episode, there was no point where his awareness left him. For this essential reason, we could, in no way, justify labels that indicated serious mental illness.

Our principal technique was simply to facilitate his own understanding of what had occurred. Ralph quite readily grasped our explanations of the release of buried stress and the resulting exhaustion and disturbance of thought and behavior. An important touch of inspiration was added to this explanation when Ralph realized that the self-awareness which he had experienced throughout his ordeal was his own true essential nature.

After a few sessions, Ralph was very knowledgeable about his recent upset, and he was determined not to push himself so hard. Because he understood how, throughout his ordeal, he had used his inner self as a solid anchor, both he and his wife were inspired to become involved in a recognized consciousness expansion program available in their area.

In facilitating understanding and insight into Ralph's problems, there is no question that we used some of the standard methods of psychoanalysis or psychotherapy. Our approach differs, however, because we do not believe it is necessary or even possible to have full or total recall of the detailed cause or nature of each stress being released.

We emphasize the importance of understanding the universal mechanics of stress release as outlined in Chapter Two, rather than intense and continuous analysis of each and every problem. As we said before, we don't have to sort through and examine each bit of junk or garbage that arises to the surface of our minds; we can simply throw it out.

UPLIFTMENT/REINFORCEMENT

Reinforcement means simply to reward behavior. It goes without saying that you are more likely to repeat an action if you expect a reward. Reinforcement is a common technique used in many forms of therapy and in fact in many forms of social interaction. For example, parents approve, reward, or actively support their children when their children engage in certain behavior, reach a desired goal, or make definite progress toward that goal.

Upliftment is a technique which uses the principle of reinforcement, but without waiting for the desired response to occur. Instead, you need to bring to the attention of the person you are helping (or to your own attention) those positive qualities, both personal and universal, which he or she possesses. This upliftment helps provide the inspiration to go forward on the road to self-fulfillment.

There are almost always numerous personal qualities about any person that can become vehicles for upliftment. Such things as concern for family, positive personal health habits, good grades in school, neat appearance and sensitivity to the environment often go unrecognized and can become sources of real gratification when they are pointed out.

The authors, for example, make it a habit to congratulate people for coming to therapy, because these people have not only become keenly aware that something is disturbing them but have taken the initiative to do something about it. This is a real display of strength, for to suffer passively is one of the worst forms of weakness.

But more importantly, we always make it a point to congratulate individuals for the more universal potentials they possess. Being born a human being is indeed a blessing in itself. Having the most sophisticated mechanism in the universe, the human nervous system, at our disposal, is surely worth mentioning, since it places us on the top rung of the ladder of physical creation. Reminding people that they own the keys to a treasure chest, pure consciousness, will almost always bring a glow. Reassuring everyone that they will surely get well in time, since life always grows and evolves to more and more, will elevate their spirits.

Most people who are evolving toward higher consciousness will respond to the reinforcement that we all have the will to choose to be anything we want to be, and we can make such a choice right now. It is a simple matter to apply reinforcement to yourself or to someone you are caring for. Keeping yourself in the company of more highly evolved, knowledgeable and inspiring people will provide exactly the right environment for reinforcement and upliftment.

We can illustrate the effectiveness of this technique with the case of Katherine. She was twenty-eight years old and had a six year history of psychological disorders, numerous stays in mental hospitals and various forms of therapy. Her list of symptoms included paranoid reactions, obsessions and phobias about dirt and gaining weight, free-floating anxiety and a negative self-image.

During the course of counseling, Katherine showed surprising awareness and insight into her own symptoms as well as a consistent desire to get well. She began to practice meditation in order to gain more awareness of her inner self, and we soon noticed that her symptoms began to decrease.

We used several techniques explained in this chapter, but the most apparent results came from reinforcement and upliftment. Over the years, Katherine had become so accustomed to her symptoms, that she could hardly see that real progress was beginning to take place even as she reported this progress. A reminder of this progress always cheered her up.

She reported frequent experiences of the Self, and when this was pointed out to her as her own true nature, she gained increasing confidence. With someone like Katherine, who had been down for so many years, an unusual amount of upliftment may be necessary. But when applied sincerely and consistently, it will bring needed and desired results.

In Katherine's case, it became easier and easier to change a sad face into a happy one. We reassured her that she could be cheerful even outside of therapy just by calling upon her own inner strength. The experience of transcendental consciousness and the release of long pent-up stresses began to gradually free her from the old symptoms.

On occasion, Katherine would display Stage III losing behavior. Then her old symptoms would reappear and she would doubt the validity of her good experiences, even question their reality, and become discouraged. But continuous reinforcement overcame her distress and lifted her to new levels of determination and wellness.

We are also reminded here of Ed, a fifty-eight year old scientist. He came to us with many of the Stage I seeking symptoms—doubt and discouragement—but with a strong underlying conviction that there was an ultimate answer to all of his doubts. Ed was a very motivated person who had made important contributions to his field of science and had also been successful in business. He had a deep respect for religion and theology, but had been unable to apply their techniques to his personal life in a way that would be satisfying to his scientific mind.

We applied the therapeutic measures of intellectual understanding and upliftment. Ed easily related to our explanation of the mechanics of stress release. Also, understanding enlightenment in terms of full human potential bridged the gap between his scientific skepticism and his spiritual needs. Ed needed to be reassured that progress was two steps forward and one step back; it was okay to make mistakes along the path. Perfection was redefined as not intentionally making mistakes, instead of not making mistakes at all.

We were also very careful to provide strong reinforcement for Ed's impressive achievements. Many people who go through Stage I seeking downgrade their past achievements for failing to deliver ultimate satisfaction. But this is a mistake. The achievements themselves may not have brought the inner peace that Ed was seeking; but neither were these achievements in any way a barrier to this inner peace.

We suggested to Ed that he should continue to take pride in his achievements because they were a sign of his developed creative intelligence. The same creative intelligence which gave rise to his past achievements could now be applied to the development of his own enlightenment. In fact, it was crying out to be applied in this way, and this was the cause of Ed's restlessness and dissatisfaction. With this understanding and reinforcement, the clouds of despair lifted from Ed's life and he proceeded to explore and find the goals he was looking for.

KEEPING A VISION OF THE GOAL

This is similar to upliftment, but with a few important distinctions. First of all, you may reinforce and uplift an individual for any number of personal achievements. But with this technique, you can point to only one vision of the goal–enlightenment, or the development of full human potential. Also, while reinforcement and upliftment can be applied as needed, the vision of the goal (for reasons we will explain) has to be applied on a frequent and consistent basis.

While reinforcement frequently is used to correct a weakness, the vision of the goal is used to correct a strength. Why does a strength need to be corrected? As we grow in consciousness, we find ourselves experiencing many benefits. Physical health radiates, senses become sharpened or "extra-sensory," and perceptions become highly refined, or even celestial. Emotions soar, and intuitions into the meaning of life abound. Super-normal powers such as knowledge of future events and the gift of healing are frequently experienced. All of these wonderful experiences can easily distract us from the goal of enlightenment.

Of course, each of these benefits is a sign of developing consciousness and a definite strength, but they are merely fringe benefits compared to the goal of enlightenment itself.

To confuse the goal with some of the benefits is to violate the traditional teachings of enlightenment and accept less from life than what we are actually capable of being. It is the confusion associated with these benefits that makes them a potential disturbance.

The ancient teachings on developing consciousness and religion are full of admonitions to avoid "side trips," however attractive, which would take us off the path to the ultimate goal. This is the reason that super-normal powers are rarely displayed in public by highly evolved persons. Such displays could easily side-track the seeker.

This does not mean that we cannot enjoy the benefits we receive in our quest for self-realization, but simply that we should not get enamored of a few trees while we lose sight of the forest. Desire, achieve, and enjoy, but in such a way as not to lose the goal. For this reason, any self-improvement program that offers less than enlightenment is limited and should be critically examined in that light.

In practice, we have found that keeping a vision of the goal can be accomplished in three steps. First, acknowledge the unusual experience that you are enjoying. Second, recognize that while the experience may be enjoyable and beneficial, it is also limited. Third, go beyond or transcend this experience.

The difficult part of this process is the second step. For many people, recognizing the enjoyable experience as just a limited gain is very sobering. Their experiences are so "flashy" they naturally want to hold on to them and enjoy them over and over again. But if they are true seekers, they will arouse themselves from this temporary trance by being reminded of the ultimate goal of enlightenment–a permanent state of consciousness, where one has become master of and gone beyond the body, senses, perception, intellect, emotions and ego.

At this stage, we are no longer just master of one power some of the time, but masters of every power anytime–beyond "becoming" and just "being." This is the vision of the goal that appeals to the finest level of every person. This is the liberation of which the great teachers and prophets throughout the ages have spoken.

Our illustration of this technique–keeping a vision of the goal–is the case of Lurene, a thirty year old woman, who became quite concerned and confused over the emergence of several super-normal powers. Increasingly, she was coming to know events prior to their occurrence. What seemed even more incredible to her, she found that she could actually influence the development of events by merely having strong desires at refined and subtle levels of thought.

Lurene was ambivalent about her super-normal powers. She was proud of herself and felt very special. But she also wondered how and why she had developed these powers. At times, she became intensely afraid of her super-normal abilities, and this caused her to be generally indecisive and easily led by others. Her ambivalence–her fear as well as her pride– came about because she could not see her powers as just a stage which she was experiencing on the path to full enlightenment.

Counseling Lurene became a matter of clearly pointing out the vision of the goal of enlightenment and helping her to put her newly emerged powers in the proper perspective. We explained the powers to her as the natural consequence of the transformation of consciousness which she was undergoing. As she was releasing stress, she was beginning to enjoy increased mind-body-environmental coordination, the basis of all super-normal powers. The power which she had particularly developed came from the fact that this coordination had grown to the point where the mind needed only to desire on a quiet, subtle level and the environment would respond with gratification of that desire. Nature responds to and supports a body and mind free of stress.

We explained to her that this power was not to be doubted. At the same time, she should not confuse it with the goal of enlightenment, but rather use the power to take her closer to the goal. This she could do by desiring life-supporting actions, including her own spiritual development. She was immediately comforted by this explanation and encouragement, and she had no trouble fitting her new found powers within the perspective of the growth of consciousness. When we saw her again after a few weeks, she once again had confidence in her decision-making powers. One of the most important ways in which she assumed responsibility for her own life was by taking active steps to make her goal of enlightenment become a reality.

DAILY ROUTINE

Having a daily routine means acting either according to a balanced internal clock or performing our important daily activities on a regular schedule according to actual clock time. All living things have their schedules or natural cycles. Plants and animals have a built-in natural instinct that tells them when to rest and be inactive and when to arise and be active. The cycles of rest and activity are natural, and man is really the only creature who needs to be reminded of this.

Of course, man has his cycles too, but these are often subject to fluctuating moods and impulses, a complex life-style and conflicting opinions and information about what is good and bad for him. All of these circumstances make it possible for us to choose a schedule of life which is unnatural and unhealthy.

It is difficult, if not impossible, to engage in an inconsistent life-style and expect at the same time that our thoughts and feelings will be consistent and balanced. The chaotic brain-wave patterns displayed by certain mental patients are powerful reminders of this reality. Our common sense and experience tell us that sooner or later we will have to pay the price for this imbalance; and this is another important illustration of the principle that every state of body has a corresponding state of mind.

Not only must we choose the amount of time we will spend resting and being active, but we must also choose carefully the quality of the rest and activity which we engage in. When our goal is to release stress, we want to be very careful to avoid activity which is stress producing. Also quite important is the need to establish a routine which we follow in a consistent manner so that our activities are not governed by our fluctuating moods.

Historically speaking, it is actually quite natural for man to follow a routine. Cultural traditions in family and village established patterns of rest and activity which were conducive to spiritual growth. But with a continuing breakdown of traditions and an increasingly rapid and changing style of living, such patterns have largely faded away. However, a regular daily routine is an adequate and necessary substitute for these patterns, especially for those undergoing a rapid transition of consciousness.

The mood swings which often accompany this transition of consciousness should not determine what we do or don't do. Just the opposite. Established daily routines of resting adequately at regular times, attending to our own spiritual growth, eating regularly and judiciously–all of these help moderate the release of stress, and make us masters of our moods rather than victims.

It has been our experience that it is surprisingly easy to introduce regularity and harmony into the lives of people who were previously lacking these qualities. Of course, individuals whose daily routines are very unbalanced, or even non-existent, will at first resist any scheduling of their time. These people first must be assured that all they are giving up is a slavish habit of their own moods. Once anyone accepts the idea of a daily routine and agrees to try it for a month, not much further convincing is necessary. Harmony and coherence become more infused in all our daily activities and this is adequate reinforcement for wanting to continue.

We applied this measure quite effectively to one of our clients, Carolyn, a twenty-three year old sailing instructor whose life had become dominated by a series of sharp mood swings. She enjoyed her work and social relationships, but this enjoyment had become almost completely overshadowed by the rapid shifts of her emotions between happiness and extreme irritability. Eventually her boyfriend tired of her irritability and the unreliability of her happy periods, and the relationship dissolved. After this, she felt helpless, insecure and out of control.

During the course of counseling, it became obvious to us that Carolyn was particularly knowledgeable about the transcendent state. We learned that her knowledge had come not from books, but from spontaneous direct experience. One of these experiences she described to us in vivid detail. While taking a walk one day, she stopped to watch some children playing. Suddenly the world seemed bathed in a golden light. She was overcome with a powerful sense of tranquility and harmony and became a silent witness not only of the activities outside of herself, but her own mental activity as well. All seemed well and wisely put.

Because of her clear and repeated experiences of the transcendent state, we concluded that her alternations of happiness and irritability were an example of Stage IV behavior, Intensification of Finding and Losing. It was unusual, but far from unique, that Carolyn had arrived at this stage without the benefit of a self-improvement program.

We found that the measure most useful in helping stabilize her mood swings was a strict adherence to a daily routine. Her former boyfriend had convinced her that continued activity was a sign of vitality and that more than six hours of sleep was a sign of laziness. Her hours for going to sleep and arising were quite irregular and she usually ate when she 'felt like it.' As soon as she structured a few more hours of sleep into her daily routine—sleep that her body needed—she experienced immediate relief.

We made out an hourly schedule of times and periods for work, play, meals, her relaxation technique, and sleep and asked Carolyn to try not to vary the routine by more than one hour. This brought an evenness to her life and in turn decreased her mood swings to a manageable level. She then realized how beneficial it was to follow a daily routine and expressed her firm resolve to continue. In a follow-up meeting, it was a joy to hear of her continued stability and progress.

"FEELING THE BODY"

"Feeling the body" may seem too simple to be called a technique, yet it is an extremely effective measure. The reason for this is that it allows the unstressing process which has already been set in motion to be completed more rapidly and more smoothly. When stresses are released, the body is being restored to its "normal" functioning power–that is, to its full potential. If the process is interfered with, resisted, or interrupted (for example through the use of tranquilizers or other drugs), the release of stress will continue, but it will take longer. Therefore, when we feel symptoms of unstressing, it is best to follow nature's orders. Simply "feel the body"; that is, allow the mind to be gently aware of any turbulence in the body and allow the intensity to subside.

Some of the physical signs of unstressing are shortness of breath, rapid heartbeat, physical sensations of heat, cold, pressure, or tingling, dizziness or faintness, and bodily tenseness or shaking. All of these may occur for no apparent reason and in the absence of any known stimulation.

The psychological correlates of physical unstressing can include free floating anxiety, a welling up of powerful feelings of sadness, disorganized thinking, sensory and perceptual distortions, and unbridled excitement. Again, these may occur without any apparent reason. This is a vast array of symptoms, but remember, we can release stress in many ways.

Motor disturbances, such as uncontrollable shaking of the body, jerking, and twitching, accompanied by rushes of energy often are present as consciousness grows. Traditionally, these experiences have been recognized and even encouraged under such names or processes as "kundalini, "opening of the chakras," "chi awakening." Regardless what name is given to these motor movements, they indicate purification of the neuropsychology, and they can be understood as unstressing. There is no more cause to be alarmed about such experiences in this situation then there is to be upset about any other spontaneous bodily reflex.

Motor disturbances of this nature indicate that the nervous system is aligning itself and something good is, indeed, happening. An important characteristic of these experiences is the lack of pain; they might be unexpected or uncomfortable, but they are merely unusual experiences of involuntary movement.

The best course of action is to allow the movements to continue without restraint, resistance, or the use of sedating or tranquilizing drugs. Understand, too, that even if the movements persist for days or weeks, they will stop in time. If at any time the movements are too intense, just open your eyes, turn your attention outward, slowly sit up, and continue "feeling the body" at a later time. Full body exercises can facilitate the process of lessening the discomfort of involuntary movement.

Whichever of these symptoms are experienced, there are two major benefits of feeling the body. First, feeling the body by allowing your attention to easily rest on the activity during periods of intense unstressing allows the mind and body to process the unstressing quickly and efficiently. Many people, during these periods of intensity, mistakenly think that the best thing to do is divert their attention to something else. This will only prolong the unstressing, which has its own natural cycle. Allow it to continue and it will work itself out. But try to stop it, and it will continue to find a disturbing way of surfacing. Putting the mind in touch with the body facilitates a natural cooperation between the two.

The second benefit of feeling the body (really a side benefit) is that the person releasing the stress will keep the process to himself or herself, without having to charge the atmosphere with negativity. Since we are mostly surrounded by people emotionally close to us, and we feel free with these people, they are the ones who end up being damaged by our release of stress. It is our friends and relatives who often bear the brunt of our anger and anxiety. Therefore, it is far better to allow our intense stress to be released gently and harmlessly while feeling the body, than displacing it onto others.

Of course, we do not use this technique every time we feel a little twitch or a touch of discomfort. We are referring here just to periods of intense unstressing. Periods of ten to fifteen minutes should be enough; even shorter if the unstressing subsides. If it is not possible to lie down, then sitting in a relaxed pose will be almost as effective.

Sometimes during severe unstressing, it is quite difficult to relax even while lying or sitting down. In this case, it is best to consciously allow the attention to easily flow to that area of the body where the greatest discomfort is located. If you are passive and neutral in this process, just allowing the bodily discomfort to get the attention of the mind, this will be a very effective technique. For a few moments, it may seem that the discomfort is actually increasing. What is really happening is that the attention is no longer diverted from the discomfort, and the calm attention of your mind toward it will allow the unstressing to be processed very quickly.

We use verbal instructions (which can be audio-taped) to help people feel their bodies. The monologue goes something like this:

> Lie down (or sit comfortably if it is impractical to lie down). Now close your eyes. Let your mind be as easy as it can be under these circumstances. What that means is don't intentionally think anything. Thoughts will come into your mind, but you don't have to start or originate them. Very innocently allow your mind's attention to go to your body.

Some physical sensation in your body will present itself to your mind. This physical sensation can come from anyplace in your body: head, feet, arms, legs, mid-section, back, chest, throat, or it may even appear to come from someplace outside or around your body. This physical sensation can be anything: pleasure, pain, hot, cold, pressure, tingling like an electric current, throbbing, dead, blocked–anything. When the sensation comes to the mind, just feel it mentally as it is.

Don't analyze the sensation; don't try to figure out what is causing it; don't try to increase or decrease it; and don't be afraid of it. Just let it come and feel it exactly as it is. If your mind takes off and you find you are thinking instead of feeling the body, gently come back to feeling the body. Feel the physical sensation in the body. If the sensation changes or goes to another part of the body, let it go and feel it. Continue this practice for ten to fifteen minutes.

The "feeling the body" technique can also become a means of facilitating deep or diaphragmatic breathing. By simply allowing the mind to "feel" yourself inhale and exhale while continuing to "watch" the process, the breath automatically becomes regular and deeper. Breathing is an autonomic (i.e., automatic) nervous system activity. Since we can hardly stop it, the less we try and the more we "feel" or "watch" ourselves breathe, the more we will benefit from the natural and deep breathing.

Another symptom of unstressing for which this technique would be very helpful is intense sexual energy or sensations. If this comes along without provocation and is quite uncomfortable, the feeling the body technique will be very helpful. Again, the most important thing is to maintain neutrality, making no attempt to either increase or decrease the sensation. You will be amazed to see how quickly this simple technique helps to lessen the disturbance. We applied this technique successfully to one of our clients, Martin, a twenty year old college student. He had come for counseling because of feelings of strong resentment toward his family, and helplessness and indecision about his vocation in life. His mind repeatedly dwelled on the environment of rejection in which he had been raised, and he was given to strong emotional outbursts.

Martin had been quite actively involved in a self-improvement program for a few years and had matured in noticeable ways. He was extremely sensitive to the needs of others, and he was recognized by his friends as being intelligent, motivated, and caring. He recognized that his current feelings of resentment and his outbursts of sobbing were due to the release of stress, but he also strongly disliked these outbursts. He was embarrassed and felt they were immature. As much as he was able, he resisted the emotional outbursts whenever they occurred.

With Martin, we recognized that some deep-rooted stresses sustained during childhood were now being released. The natural conclusion was to allow this process to continue until it was completed. It would have been useless and even harmful to bring up too much of the past or probe the unconscious regarding childhood events, since these disturbances were already being released. It was much better for all concerned to adopt an attitude of calm acceptance of the ongoing process.

With regard to the emotional outbursts, we asked Martin to lie down whenever they occurred, and to be aware of the bodily disturbances which accompanied these outbursts. After he did this a few times, the outbursts started to become considerably less intense, and this in turn lessened Martin's fear of "hidden ghosts" within himself. In these cases, allowing is much better for growth than resisting.

With this success behind him, he courageously turned to the task of allowing his personality to unfold on the basis of his inner core, which he knew from experience to be the Self. Follow-up meetings revealed that he had taken definite steps toward a satisfactory career and was more accepting of his family and himself.

INTENSE PHYSICAL EXERCISE

We have seen that deep rest is a necessity for the rapid evolution of consciousness. Also important is intense physical activity. This is a technique which needs to be emphasized for those on the path to higher consciousness. Of course, we only begin intensive physical exercises after consulting a medical professional.

We know that numerous self-improvement programs available in our day offer deep rest as a means of stilling the mind and experiencing the unmoving, non-active state of transcendental consciousness. This deep rest is facilitated by techniques such as meditation, biofeedback, prayer, chanting, and contemplation. Some have found it possible to experience that silent basis of life somewhat spontaneously, without any technique.

In any case the deep rest is there and must be matched by intense activity. This is not to satisfy some abstract and vague idea of balance, but for a scientific reason. From a psychological perspective what is happening is that the deep rest releases stress from the subtle areas within the nervous system. When it is released, the stress must pass through the physical structures of the body (chemical, muscular, etc.) in order to be dissipated. The nervous system, which includes the more subtle components of the brain and spinal column, releases the stress into the body including the glands and muscles. It is on this grosser, external level of glands and muscles that intense physical activity is required in order to facilitate stress release.

Attached to many self-improvement programs are numerous systems of slow physical exercise, which work to calm the subtle body. These activities include breathing exercises, yoga, tai-chi and others. They are all beneficial supplements to self-improvement programs and may even serve as such programs in and of themselves.

However, it has been our experience that these activities, while definitely worthwhile, are much too subtle to meet the immediate therapeutic need of gross stress release. Additionally, these techniques can, and often do, increase unstressing, rather than decrease or moderate it, thereby compounding the problem. What is needed is activity that meets head-on the stress release that is taking place on the muscular and glandular level.

For this reason, we highly recommend intense physical exercise as a part of any self-improvement program. By this we mean exercise that stimulates the cardiovascular system (remember, the heart is a muscle), requires muscular strength, and demands gradually increasing coordination, strength and flexibility to execute. There are many exercise programs and activities that meet these requirements, including tennis, jogging, aerobics, swimming, brisk walks and workouts on scientifically designed body-building machines.

Intense exercise is applicable to a wide range of unstressing symptoms and of particular benefit to individuals who get angry very easily, experience fatigue, have low motivation, lack confidence, and who exhibit rapid mood swings. People who display these symptoms are generally not self-motivated to begin a program of intense exercise, so they must be encouraged. They may resist the first few workouts, but after a couple of weeks the benefits are evident, including better sleep, more confidence, less irritability and a general sense of well being. It is interesting to note that studies in physiology show that exercise increases energy and lessens fatigue, rather than wearing a person out, as was commonly thought.

Our illustration for this technique is the case of Sam, a forty-two year old professional. Sam had been involved in spiritual pursuits for a number of years and he was proud of the fact that he took very good care of himself. He was careful about what he ate, he looked trim and he regularly practiced a program of yoga exercises to go along with his spiritual program.

Despite all this, he felt very passive, with no motivation to go to work or continue to achieve. Intellectually, he wanted to continue to do well at work and continue his life-long habit of learning and growing. But emotionally and physically, he often felt stuck and had to push himself very hard to go on achieving.

When we first suggested exercise to him as a way to combat his passivity, he was quite resistant. He felt he was in good health and was already following the correct regimen for his body. He said that intense physical exercise was too gross and would adversely affect the quiet and calm state of mind and body that he was trying to achieve. But when we explained the mechanics of stress release in relation to his particular case, and that exercise would supplement and not undermine his present program, he agreed to enroll in a structured exercise program.

The positive results were apparent within a month. His moods stabilized, his will power became stronger and the passivity almost disappeared. Far from destroying his inner subtlety, he found that the exercise helped him to maintain his self-awareness by preventing his inner Self from being over-shadowed by dark moods and periods of indecision.

AFFIRMATIONS

Perhaps you have heard the expression, "You are what you eat?" Certainly this has much truth to it, especially on the physical level. Poor nutrition leads to poor health, and good nutrition is conducive to good health.

But if it is true that we are what we eat, then how much truer it is to say that we are what we think. There is ample evidence from the field of psychology to show that a positive self-concept results in a healthy, strong and productive life, while a negative self-concept results in a downward spiral toward illness, loss of confidence, depression and inertia. Our personal systems of belief are self-fulfilling prophecies, producing positive or negative results, depending on our expectations.

As early as the turn of the century, one of the first Americans in the field of psychology, William James, recognized that habits have their corresponding pathways in the neuro-physiology. When we start to form a habit, it is like clearing a path in the woods. The longer we have the habit, the more well-worn the path becomes. Pretty soon the path widens into a road, and it is the only road we know how to take. We travel it over and over, even though the circumstances of our life may have changed, and we may actually have very good reasons for forming new and better habits.

The conflict between old habits and new growth is the cause of a common disturbance accompanying the growth of consciousness. People have come to us feeling that the very foundation of their lives has improved quite radically, yet they complain that some of their mental patterns of self-defeat and despair have not changed at all.

For these people, we use the analogy of the audiotape. A poor, unhappy and unhealthy person may get up every morning and listen to the same tape about his terrible condition (a tape, by the way, which he himself recorded). When he makes a change for the better, he finds that his progress is thwarted by the old tape, which he feels bound to listen to day in and day out. Even if he has laid a solid foundation for a life of health and happiness, he may find that he cannot build upon this foundation. The message of the old tape keeps pulling him down.

When we look at it through the perspective of this analogy, then changing the habit of negative thought is as easy as changing a cassette on the tape machine. We need to begin the process of a new and positive thought pattern by putting on a new tape. We soon become accustomed to the message of the new tape, and the message of the old tape becomes foreign. This is what the technique of affirmation does–it creates a new, positive mode of thinking which subsequently forms the basis for positive action.

Practically speaking, the first step in the affirmation process is to determine the negative or irrational thoughts that are coloring your feelings and behavior. These thoughts usually emerge quite naturally or with some gentle probing during any discussion about your unpleasant feelings. Some of the most common are: "I should be better than I am"; "I am not good enough"; "I am not doing (or didn't do) well enough";

"I should be doing better than I am (or did)." Also common are such negative or irrational thoughts as "Nothing I do makes any difference"; "I can never do anything right"; "I'll never find a job or meet the right mate."

Once you are able to isolate the troubling or irrational thought, the process of creating an affirmation becomes a simple matter. Now you can come up with a statement that is as close to the original, but without the negative or irrational words such as "should," "ought," "must," "never," or "always." In this way you are substituting positive, highly charged, rational words for negative, draining, irrational thoughts. Thus, "I should be better than I am" becomes "I am who I am and I'm OK (despite my imperfections and no matter what anybody says about me)." Another affirmation we use frequently is: "I'm doing (or did) the best that I can and it's OK, no matter how it turns out." Similarly, the negative thought, "Nothing I do makes any difference" becomes "Everything I do has some reason and importance."

When we counsel people, we take special care to prescribe a clear, positively worded affirmation without if's or but's. Special care is also taken to follow the words "I am", a powerful self statement, with something positive and rational. We have the person write down the affirmation and then rehearse it out loud a few times. We then instruct the individual to begin each day by actually writing the affirmation down ten times and to briefly think the affirmation anytime it happens to come to mind throughout the day. Writing it down allows the person to use the message as the basis for that day's activities; and dwelling on it for a few seconds whenever it happens to occur provides periodic reinforcement.

An alternate instruction, which is particularly effective if you are practicing a mental quieting technique such as meditation or biofeedback, is to repeat the affirmation silently several times _after_ you finish your mental technique. Just as a photograph is clearer and the impressions richer when the camera is held steady, so the mind is more receptive after you have settled it down.

We also instruct people who are repeating an affirmation, either mentally or in writing, to feel it emotionally and dare to believe it. Even if you only make the affirmation truly yours for a moment, you have begun the process of transformation. Because emotions operate on a subtler and more powerful level than the intellect, this momentary feeling of ownership for the affirmation helps to deepen its impression.

Initially the affirmation, like other techniques here, may meet with resistance. Many people will insist that the content of the affirmation is just not so, it doesn't match the facts of their lives, and they feel hypocritical repeating it. We sympathize with these objections. However, when people report growth of consciousness, then we feel perfectly justified in trying to erase a habit of thought that arose from a less developed level of consciousness, and then replacing it with thought and action more appropriate to their new-found inner growth.

For these reasons, we have no hesitation in extracting from our clients a promise to carry out the simple instructions regardless of what they believe and feel. If you are doing this for yourself, you need simply to promise yourself you will do it, at least for a few weeks, no matter how you feel about it. Once the analogy of the tape recording is understood and the promise is given to at least try the affirmation, then there is a foothold which can only lead you further along the path of positivity.

The experience of most people practicing the affirmation technique is that repeating the affirmation eventually becomes much more attractive than they could have imagined. This is understandable, since the nature of the mind is to grow towards more and more fulfillment, and affirmation provides nourishment for this growth.

After two or three weeks, the affirmation no longer feels foreign, and the person feels that he or she begins to "own" the positive or more rational thought. When this feeling of real ownership occurs, noticeable changes in mood and behavior occur. The affirmation is now "programmed" in and will automatically operate whenever it needs to–during the exact same circumstances that previously provoked the negative response.

It is simply a process of mental conditioning, just like physical conditioning where you break down fat and develop muscle. Once the new habit of thinking is completely learned, there is no longer any need to repeat the affirmation. The new habit will be self-reinforcing as soon as we experience the first positive results. Since it makes us feel good and those around us will also appreciate it, we are sure to continue our new positive behavior.

As we have indicated, the affirmation technique will be most effective with people who have had some experience of transcendental consciousness. When we have this experience, old negative habits seem out of place and our underlying instinct is to get rid of them. Also, the consistent release of stress makes us more flexible and less resistant to change; we become particularly receptive to new learning and open to major changes in attitude. As we begin to experience the most profound layers of consciousness, then whatever we put our attention on will grow stronger in our lives.

We applied the affirmation technique very effectively with Gregg, a forty-eight year old educator. Gregg had participated in consciousness-raising programs for over twelve years, and he was quite pleased with the results on the level of both understanding and experience. However, he was still plagued by social anxiety, which took the form of nervousness, inhibition, and awkwardness whenever he had to speak before a group (other than the classroom) or mix with strangers at a social function. Gregg found this most disagreeable, especially since the rest of his life was going so well. Although he got through these occasions reasonably well and without anyone else noticing his discomfort, eventually he got down on himself for not having performed better.

He tried a number of measures to correct his fear, such as breathing exercises and joining a speakers' club. He relentlessly pursued every opportunity to speak or socialize in an attempt to confront his fear, rather than avoid it. None of these measures brought any real relief. Naturally, he felt quite discouraged, and he even began to doubt the effectiveness of the consciousness expansion program to which he had devoted himself.

In the course of counseling, Gregg revealed that he had been an only, but happy, child and that he was always somewhat introverted. Married, but with a few close friends including his wife, he still enjoyed being alone frequently. He genuinely did not like public-speaking or social functions, and he really did not want to engage in them. But Gregg admitted that inside himself he was playing an old tape—one that said he "wasn't good enough," and that he "should be a dynamic speaker and socializer." Gregg simply was not accepting himself as he was, and this non-acceptance prevented him from being himself with others.

Rather than attempt to change his basic personality (a futile gesture anyway) or add yet another skills improvement technique to Gregg's agenda, we recommended that he practice a fundamental ego affirmation. We suggested, "I am who I am and that's all I am right now, and I'm OK, no matter what anybody thinks or says." We instructed Gregg to write the affirmation down ten times a day and to think–and dare to believe–and to feel the affirmation for a few seconds several times after his daily meditation. After one week, Gregg reported that the affirmation was less foreign to him, and it frequently occurred to him during the day. He had even begun to like it.

Gradually and quite spontaneously over the next few weeks, Gregg's confidence and ease in social situations improved. He allowed himself to be rather quiet and retiring, but now he accepted himself as such. He still spoke before groups, but only when necessary, and he noticed that he did so with much more ease and less need to impress others. In fact, he felt freer to self-disclose more with others. The affirmation seemed to go to the very core of Gregg's ego or self-concept. We were impressed with the rapid progress Gregg made–a rapidity which we attributed to his highly evolved mind-body coordination.

DAILY ACT OF THE WILL

This technique is similar to the affirmation technique. The difference is that while affirmation directly involves thought, the daily act of the will directly involves action. The person using this technique simply performs one or more activities each day that he or she would not ordinarily do. The activity should be simple and beneficial to themselves or another person and need not take longer than five or ten minutes. Each time the action is performed, it should be written down in a sentence or two in a journal, as an indication of our progress. The activity could be something as simple as a telephone call to a friend, straightening out the closet, or reading a book–anything positive.

This technique is particularly helpful for persons who display Stage III, (Temporary Losing) behavior, such as indecision, procrastination, and the feeling of being helpless or out of control of their lives. We generally explain to people that the will is like a muscle. If it is exercised, it becomes strong and responsive; if not, it turns flabby and inactive.

Through misunderstanding about the will, people undergoing a transformation of consciousness often fail to properly exercise their will power. That is, they temporarily cease making positive, direct decisions and they become progressively weaker. These people mistakenly relinquish their will to such ideas as "God takes care of his own," "Relax and accept what comes to you," or "The universe will support me." None of these was ever meant to imply that we are required to do nothing on our part. Nevertheless, this is what many seekers think they need to do–nothing. This is an attitude which will undermine the gains they have enjoyed and bring on feelings of hopelessness and helplessness.

We have also found this condition in others, who, having experienced the Self, long for the experience again; and not finding satisfaction after repeated "attempts," (probably forcing the situation rather than relaxing) they conclude that "Since nothing I do makes any difference, then that's what I'll do–nothing." Such an attitude can immobilize us and induce a state of depression.

We all need to know that the will is not a useless appendage, but an essential part of our humanity, one which sets us apart from other living things. Will is free to the extent that we can choose which action to follow, and not free to the extent that the results of the action we perform are influenced by natural or social forces already in operation. For this reason, existential philosophers have stated that man is only human when he is choosing; in exercising his free will, he is performing a uniquely human function.

You are only free and responsible for initiating the right action, but not for the results of the action, which are out of your control. We take special care to emphasize this as our definition of free will. In other words, you do what you think is right, and then you let it go. You expect nothing; and accept everything. Attachment to the results or fruits of your action, as the age old wisdom states, will keep you longer on the wheel of ignorance.

In the state of enlightenment, our choices are automatically in accord with the highest laws of nature, and human and divine will are one and the same. But until we reach that state, and in fact in order to reach that state, we must act and make correct choices.

Each action that is positive takes us closer to the goal. Positive actions are those which are life supporting and which we know to be right. If we have lost track of what is right, we can follow our tradition, the law of the land, our religion or the teachings of wise persons throughout the ages.

On the other hand, negative actions sidetrack us and take us further from the goal. And inaction, paralysis of the will, stops us dead in our tracks. Correct understanding of the function of the will and a daily act of the will facilitate our ability to be motivated and self-starting, and help us to make steady progress toward our goal of enlightenment.

The effectiveness of using will power is illustrated in the case of Martha, a twenty-seven year old waitress. She had two Masters degrees, and she came to us for counseling because of feelings of discouragement and a lack of vocational purpose. She said that her interests were continually changing and as a result she could never seriously devote herself to a long-term career. At the same time she was very upset about this because she knew how talented and intelligent she was.

Her frustration about her inability to make this important career decision was like a cancer which spread out and affected her ability to act or speak even on the smallest issue. She had no doubt about her own self worth, and she understood that her current frustration was at least partly due to a rapid transition in consciousness and the resulting release of stress. Still, she felt unable to push the start button in her life, so that her many talents would blossom.

We applied several of the techniques explained in this chapter, but the most useful was the daily act of the will. We made a list of several small activities which would be beneficial for her to accomplish. We instructed her to complete two of these activities everyday and report back to us in a week. By accomplishing these small tasks, she began to exercise her will, and in doing so she became increasingly in charge of her life and confident that she could accomplish whatever she wanted. Sure enough, within three months, she began a job for which her education had prepared her and was looking beyond to her first promotion.

If you are unemployed or out of school because you aren't sure what you want to do with your life, we always advise active involvement in some type of job or educational pursuit. Because active involvement establishes a basis for achievement and self-confidence, it is better to do something rather than nothing. Find a job or a course of study; almost anything will do. Stay with it until something better or more appealing is available; then change. Consider this course of action very much like getting into the main stream of your life. If you stand on the shore and wait, you go nowhere. If you get in at the shoreline repeatedly, eventually you will find the ripple or current that will take you to the center where the flow will carry you along effortlessly.

INTERPERSONAL COMMUNICATION SKILLS

Effective interpersonal skills means the ability to interact with other people in an easy and natural way. Everyone needs these skills, but they can be of special benefit to persons undergoing a rapid transformation of consciousness. These persons often misunderstand others, and may themselves be misunderstood and socially rejected for reasons associated with the stages in the growth of consciousness. The fanaticism found in Stage II, Temporary Finding, the procrastination and helplessness in Stage III, Temporary Losing, and the rapid mood swings of Stage IV, Intensification of Finding and Losing, are some of the reasons for misunderstanding and the breakdown of effective communication. The inability to communicate and the feeling of isolation further aggravate the psychological disturbances.

Mastering effective interpersonal skills can go a long way toward overcoming these barriers to smooth growth. As with all skills, the learning involves practice. There are a number of situations in which you can experiment with new styles of interpersonal communication and also get valuable feedback from others. The most obvious laboratory is in your home, where you may try out new behaviors that facilitate harmonious relationships between you and your friends and family members.

Another good laboratory is often provided in special group activities sponsored by schools, churches, social service agencies, and fraternal and private organizations. These include human relations training groups, leadership training groups, assertiveness training and many other types of communication workshops. Any of these groups provides an environment where you can safely experiment with new styles of communication.

However, it is best to avoid high-pressure encounter groups which apply harsh and unnatural measures (lack of sleep, strong group persuasion, etc.) in order to make you disclose inner fears or anxieties. For reasons we've explained, such disclosures will be useless or even harmful for someone in your situation. It is much healthier to join a group which fosters frank discussion through loving encouragement.

We will now discuss four of the most effective communication skills for persons on the path to higher consciousness.

1. Listening

People who come into possession of a profound knowledge about the meaning of life are naturally eager to share their new insights with people they know and sometimes with society in general. This is an admirable ambition, but in practice it can lead to a self-centered zealousness. As a result, communication becomes one-sided, with the other person effectively barred from making any contribution at all to the discussion. In this case, we can hardly use the word "discussion," since the message is falling on deaf ears. In a real discussion, people actively listen and respond to one another.

Respect for others and active listening are necessary for real two-way communication. And if you feel that you have an important message to get across, then active listening can pinpoint what is lacking in another person's understanding and provide an opportunity to direct a few well chosen and well placed words. This will be far more effective than a lengthy one-sided lecture.

Also, when we listen, we learn and grow. We should be attentive not just to another person's words, but to their age, their position in life and their achievements. Especially when attempting to communicate with someone much older than us, or in a higher position, it is much better to take the approach, "Please let me share with you what I have learned," rather than, "Let me teach you." By truly listening and respecting, we culture our emotions of love and sharing, and break down isolating barriers.

2. Cooperation, Acceptance, and Compassion

In certain areas of life, such as athletics, competition is unavoidable. There must be winners and losers. But in communication, especially related to the growth of consciousness, it is not necessary for anyone to be a loser. In this area, being a winner is the birthright of every human being. In fact, when good communications take place there can only be winners. An attitude of spiritual pride and one-upsmanship only serves to make others feel hostile and diminished rather than motivated to actualize his or her highest potential.

For the sake of our own personal evolution, and also for the sake of planetary transformation, we should recognize that every person begins his or her quest for enlightenment from whatever level of consciousness that person is experiencing at the time. You cannot judge others by the experiences or insights which you have enjoyed, just as you would not wish to be judged by the experiences of other people. Judgment and competitiveness, rather than cooperation and compassion, will tend to isolate you and make others feel increasingly unable or unwilling to communicate with you.

In our practice, we have seen competitive and judgmental people whose lack of compassion has come back to haunt them. The path to enlightenment is marked by high and low points, and a person feeling on top of the world may suddenly find himself plunged rudely back to earth. When this occurs, any feelings of judgment we have had make our present disturbance even more bitter, because we begin to apply the same harsh criticism to ourselves.

When we get beneath critical, judgmental behavior, most frequently what we find is an arrested or incomplete self-concept or ego. People who lack self-acceptance and have a deep rooted sense of inferiority often unconsciously project this deficiency. They outwardly criticize others in order to defend themselves.

Through an understanding of the mechanics of stress release, we know that seekers after enlightenment unstress deeply. During this unstressing, their defense mechanisms fall away, exposing an ego which, for so long, they have erroneously identified as their true nature. Because of this erroneous identification, often they vigorously engage in a last ditch defensive effort to protect egos, in fact, that were conditioned by their past weaknesses. Fortunately, their awareness is also on the rise. A gentle reminder for acceptance of and compassion for others may be all that is needed to bring tears to their eyes and the blessed relief that comes when they stop the process of condemnation or self or others.

Another important distinction needs to be made. When you accept yourself or others, it does not necessarily mean that you like or agree with every thought, feeling, or behavior that is manifested. To accept simply means to recognize what is–without judgement.

3. Disclosure of Feeling

When psychological disturbances accompany the growth of consciousness: we are often afraid to disclose our true feelings. This fear is generally fueled by the mistaken ideas that: 1) emotion is inferior to intellect, and 2) "normal" behavior is devoid of any expression of negative emotion.

These ideas arise out of the laudable intentions of self-improvement organizations, which exaggerate the importance of keeping our thoughts, speech, and behavior positive. Adherents of these organizations begin to develop a fear of rejection if they openly express fears, resentments, doubts or other negative emotions.

Certainly, it is better to cultivate positive emotions and display positive behavior, but when we experience strong negative emotions, it does little good to deny, resist, or suppress these feelings. This suppression brings about a condition recognized by psychologists as incongruity–meaning imbalance between internal feelings and external behavior. The result of this incongruity is artificial mood making, uptightness, plastic emotions, aloofness, and a lack of empathy and human caring. Incongruity blocks the natural flow of behavior and growth.

By disclosure of feelings, we do not mean unrestricted public self-disclosure. Tirades and tantrums will confuse those with whom we are trying to communicate, and aggravate the internal pressure we are experiencing. Healthy expression of feelings means that in the quiet hours we spend with friends, relatives, or a counselor, we feel free to share our feelings, both positive and negative. If we cannot be honest with ourselves and with these people, then our energy will be spent on blocking feelings, rather than where it should be spent—on growing toward the fullness of life.

In short, it is better to dwell on the positive. But, as the natural consequence of the release of stress, you are almost sure to have negative feelings. When this happens and it seems to be just a passing thing, we can just let it pass, or, if it is intense, try the feeling the body technique suggested earlier. But if the feeling persists, then seek out someone you feel comfortable with. Everyone undergoing a transformation of consciousness should have at least one or two confidants who can listen to the free expression of feeling in a loving and non-judgmental way.

If you find yourself having rather dramatic experiences or you are in possession of some super-normal powers, assume a low profile for a while. It is best not to broadcast your experiences or draw attention to yourself. Doing so could confuse others, and increase their social rejection of you. Initially, share your feelings only with selected individuals who you are confident will understand or are in a position to help you. Go about your business as usual while keeping centered on the growth of consciousness within. In time, any disturbance regarding your new experiences will pass.

4. Assertiveness
Assertiveness is necessary to complement the other communication techniques because it is sometimes necessary to be an active and outspoken participant in the communications process. On the path to enlightenment our apparent and observed

behavior may not seem up to par with our cherished and lofty goals. Unfortunately, those around us are often all too ready to criticize and abuse us for this disparity. In addition, because we ourselves recognize this disparity and are often our own worst critics, we may feel we deserve other people's abuse. This will be especially frustrating if we are already experiencing the doubt and discouragement of Stage III losing behavior.

In this case, the most helpful communication skill to use is assertiveness, or confrontation. Whenever we find ourselves unjustly criticized, the victim of unreasonable/abusive behavior, or we see an obvious flaw in someone else's opinion, we should stand up for ourselves and clearly state our position.

This does not mean an open opportunity to act irresponsibly and vindictively. It should be welcomed as a chance to involve yourself with someone else and to carefully review the issue of your own development. The basic attitude is caring—caring that a conflict is resolved, caring about what the other person has to say, and caring about your own self-esteem.

Frank confrontation releases pent up frustrations, clears the air, reinforces our beliefs, and strengthens our resolve to make progress toward full spiritual growth. It is interesting to note that acting assertively has been found to activate an area of the brain which at the same time inhibits anxiety. It has also been shown to be a definite confidence builder.

Remember that there is a definite difference between assertiveness and attack. Uncontrolled anger will only trigger more angry outbursts. Just assume the position that rather than attack or retreat from the confrontation, you will accept it openly as an opportunity for self-examination and involvement. Above all, have the courage to speak out what you know to be right, even if you are not yet living it.

Many people who come to see us need assertiveness training, which may involve role-playing and real-life practice. There are numerous well-written books available on assertiveness. Also in most communities, you can find courses offered from time to time which teach assertiveness skills. Above all, don't wait to be self-confident before you begin to assert yourself–assert first, and then you will become more self-confident. Remember what we said at the beginning of Chapter Four: a strong individuated self or ego must be established before you can transcend completely. Assertiveness facilitates this process.

Each of these four techniques has its place in different situations. The time to be assertive is not when a loving and caring friend is trying to help you express your true feelings. And the time to listen patiently is not when another person is roundly abusing you. It will be obvious to you which situation is appropriate for which communication skill.

Our illustration of the effectiveness of open communication is the case of Nick, a young man who was relentless in pursuing his own personal goal of enlightenment and equally zealous in attempting to share his knowledge with others. Quite unexpectedly he became involved in a romantic relationship. His girl friend, while not as spiritually astute as Nick, was nevertheless much more emotionally mature. Lovingly, but quite candidly, she pointed out to him how out of touch he was with his own feelings and how little he had done in his life to cultivate emotions of love and tenderness.

Subsequently, when the relationship dissolved, Nick was very disturbed at his inability to relate to others in an open, honest and warm manner. He developed new insights into himself which he wanted to share with his friends, but he was unable to do so because of fear of censure and rejection by the organization he belonged to. As is often the case, he became increasingly imprisoned by self-imposed sanctions which were not even a part of the teachings he had received. He withdrew into himself until he could barely tolerate it. One day, a friend in the same organization casually asked Nick how he was feeling. Hardly thinking, Nick blurted out, "I feel awful." Strangely enough, the friend replied, "So do I," at which time both friends took the opportunity to express their heartfelt, honest feelings to each other.

Nick remembered this incident as a turning point in his interpersonal relations. Once he was able to honestly express his feelings, then in turn he found his attitude toward others more accepting. He began to study the works of several great humanistic psychologists, an interest he had previously denied himself because he felt that his own organization provided the complete explanation of human behavior. From his readings, he began to understand and change several aspects of his communication style which had long given him difficulty. One of these was his fanatical behavior.

Nick still maintained a healthy respect for his self-improvement program and continued to adhere to its practices, but not blindly as before. He was eager to explore and express mature emotions, and he willingly participated in the human relations training group which we suggested to him. In our counseling we simply verified and reinforced Nick's discovery of how necessary the natural expression of feeling is.

——————— ✧ ———————

This concludes our presentation of the various therapeutic techniques. As a graphic summary, we include a table which matches the symptoms preceding the initial enlightenment experience with the treatments described in this chapter. As you can see from the table, each symptom matches more than one treatment, and some treatments can be applied to every one of the symptoms. We have indicated with stars (★) the treatments which we have found to be most helpful for each symptom.

This clear and simple approach to the treatments is one which we heartily recommend, since the treatments can easily be self-applied. It is our experience that most individuals undergoing a rapid growth toward higher consciousness are very aware of their own behavior, self-motivated and willing to learn to help themselves. Of course, there will always be individuals who, for different reasons, will need some help in applying these techniques, and these people should seek out a sympathetic counselor. If you are choosing a counselor, be strong in your convictions and resist counseling which attempts to undermine your own spiritual goals. Ideally, counseling or therapy should be a short-term affair.

There will also be those individuals whose difficulties will require referral to an appropriate professional. These situations are discussed in detail in Appendix A "When To Seek Outside Help."

The treatments we have offered are largely psychological. There are also numerous treatments of a physical nature offered by health professionals which have potential value in treating the psychological disturbances accompanying the growth of consciousness. These include nutrition, fasting, vitamins, massage, body work, acupuncture, spinal adjustment, and many others found under the heading of holistic medicine.

TABLE OF SYMPTOMS AND TECHNIQUES

SYMPTOMS	TECHNIQUES								
	Intellectual Understanding	Upliftment and Reinforcement	Keeping Vision of the Goal	Daily Routine	Feeling the Body	Intense Physical Exercise	Affirmations	Daily Act of the Will	Interpersonal Communication Skills
Dissatisfaction, Meaninglessness and Seeking	x	x	✪						
Emotional Flooding	x	x	x	x	✪	x			
Ego Inflation - Fanaticism	✪	x	x	x	x	x			✪
Doubt, Discouragement and Cynicism	x	✪	x	x		x	x	x	
Resentment and Anger	x	x	x	x	x	✪		x	x
Ego Deflation, Helplessness, Indecision, Procrastination	x	x	x	x	x	✪	x	✪	x
Sensory-Motor-Perceptual Disturbances	✪	x	x	x	✪	x			
Accelerated Mood Swings	x	x	x	✪	x	✪	x		
Ego Identity Conflicts	✪	x	x	x	x	x	✪		
Intellectual Confusion	✪	x	x						
Social Rejection/ Communication Difficulties	x	x					x		✪
Witnessing or "Out of the Body" Experiences	✪	x	x	x	x	x			

x – Indicates an appropriate treatment for symptoms described.
✪ – Indicates most commonly effective treatment for the symptoms described.

137

Appendix A
When To Seek Outside Help

Our purpose in this book has been to help you as you guide yourself on the path to fulfillment and enlightenment. However, it is important to know that there may be disturbances accompanying the growth of consciousness which are too jarring or too severe to be handled without assistance from a professional resource. Likewise, there may be severe disturbances which cannot be attributed only to the purifying effects of the spiritual path in which you are participating.

Also, it may very well be that the spiritual or growth movement in which you participate does not readily admit to these possibilities. Among many growth and spiritual movements, there exists the belief that the techniques and knowledge which they offer are completely sufficient and all that a follower will ever need. Such beliefs are generally well-intentioned and perhaps true on a metaphysical or ultimate level. But on a practical, every-day level, they have often proven to be naive. Every movement or group has had its share of individuals whose difficulties become unmanageable.

Many of these situations have had tragic results for the individuals involved.

Therefore, just as it is a mistake **not** to recognize disturbances accompanying the growth of consciousness, it is also a mistake **not** to recognize when you need help beyond your own ability or the ability and understanding of a group, movement, or its leaders. There is no shame in calling on a skilled and understanding professional for mental, social, or physical assistance; such assistance does not diminish the value of your own quest for fulfillment.

For this reason, we are identifying four critical situations when referral to a professional individual or agency would be especially appropriate.

1. Psychosis

As we discussed in Chapter One, essentially psychosis is the loss of contact with reality or the loss of self-awareness. Psychosis is most frequently accompanied by either disorientation with regard to time, place, or person, or by hallucinations or delusions.

Hallucinations are experiences of sights, sounds, voices, touches, tastes, or smells that are not experienced by anyone else present. In these cases, the individual is not "witnessing" or reflecting on the experiences, but is in fact fully identified with them and believes they are taking place. Any questioning of the experiences by others is usually met with confusion, disbelief, and resistance. For example, a person claims that he hears or sees angels singing, but can not understand or accept that no one else hears or sees them, because he believes it is an objective experience.

Another sign of psychosis relates to bizarre delusions of either persecution or grandeur. A person, without the slightest recognition that the delusions are coming from fear, might believe without any basis in fact that he is being punished or sought out. For example, this individual might suspect that CIA and FBI agents are following him around day and night and watching everything he does. The suggestion that this might be unwarranted is met with disbelief or hostility. In the case of delusions of grandeur, someone claims that he is the "Messiah" or "Almighty One," without any recognition that his body or personality is mortal or limited in nature.

The flag of caution should be raised also in the case of manic/depressive behaviors. Examples are rapid and unrelated progression of ideas, speech, planning, or action; sleeplessness; extreme excitement, agitation, buying or planning sprees, and sexual indiscretions–all without awareness of their consequences. Prolonged, disoriented, morbid, or vegetative depression with no insight or desire for relief are other signs of serious mental illness.

In any event, prompt referral to a psychiatrist, licensed psychologist, mental health clinic, or hospital is clearly in order for any of these symptoms described. Drugs and/or hospitalization are currently the "state of the art" in these cases, and we recommend compliance with these treatments until something better is available.

However, since a wide range of sensory, motor, perceptual, and mood disturbances can accompany the growth of consciousness, care must be taken not to identify every disturbance as psychotic. Following are simple criteria to determine the difference:

Length of the Disturbance–Generally disturbances accompanying the growth of consciousness persist only for brief periods of time–usually a few days.

Consistency of the Disturbance–The appearance and disappearance, or the waxing and waning of disturbances are usually signs of manageable stress release. When the symptoms are constant and extend over time, they are indicative of more serious psychopathology.

"Witnessing" the Disturbance–If the person can reflect upon the disturbance by talking about it, admitting its unusualness, understanding its possible source and course, seeing it as a by-product of stress release, and agreeing to practice some of the stabilization techniques discussed in this book, then the likelihood of psychosis is remote. "Witnessing" or awareness of the symptomology is the most important criteria.

————◇————

In cases of heavy unstressing or panic-like feelings which are clearly not psychosis, we have frequently noted that small amounts of alcohol or prescribed tranquilizers administered on a one-time or very limited basis have ended or neutralized particularly disturbing periods of heavy unstressing. This measure can be taken after the techniques mentioned in Chapter Five (particularly feeling the body with attention to breathing) have been attempted without result. It is not our practice or position to recommend or prescribe drugs or alcohol; but it seems that what has happened in these situations is that the gross effect of the substances have erased some of the subtle effects of the spiritual technique which the person is practicing. In doing so, it may also have put a halt to the deeper process of unstressing and may thus have given some temporary but necessary relief. If the panic-like feelings continue, consult a mental health professional.

2. Suicide Risk

If you are in the position of advising a friend, fellow seeker, or follower, it is important for you to recognize when a person is at genuine risk for suicide. As a rule, fleeting or casual talks of suicide are not in themselves sufficient to determine serious risk for suicide. However, when thoughts or expressions of suicide are accompanied by one or more of the following situations, the possibility of a suicide attempt needs to be taken very seriously.

a. Clear intent to commit suicide is openly expressed.

b. Concrete plans for suicide are devised and revealed.

c. Specific lethal means such as guns or hanging are considered.

d. A history of previous suicide attempts exists.

e. The person engages in suicidal behavior, such as writing a suicide note or giving favorite things away.

f. The person exhibits impulsive behavior, such as quitting a job, running away, overdosing on drugs or alcohol, or displaying inappropriate and intense anger or rage.

g. A history of drug and alcohol abuse exists.

h. The person lacks a support system or supportive people in their life.

i. A recent crisis was experienced, such as death of a loved one, separation, divorce, arrest, loss of job, income, or home.

j. There is a history of depression or the recent lifting of a depression.

Again, we emphasize that contact with and referral to a licensed mental health professional or suicide prevention agency are necessary. This time, however, the referral needs to be immediate. The referred agency will advise whether it is also necessary to notify family or friends.

Let us hasten to point out that we do not believe suicide or any other of the critical situations which we deal with here are necessary by-products or results of engaging in genuine growth practices, or self-help techniques. Problems do erupt, however, when the ideal of a growth or spiritual movement—to take the burden of the world on its own shoulders–is overshadowed by the fact that people sometimes bring to the movement very troubled personal histories. As we have said, when there is a failure to recognize that such a troubled history may be outside of the ability of the movement or group to handle, the results could be tragic.

3. Serious or Threatening Physical Health Ailments

Individuals with physical complications should not undertake or continue with a technique or program that facilitates heavy unstressing without consulting a physician. This is clearly in keeping with the common sense precaution regarding most rigorous activities by anyone with physical complications. Heart conditions, high blood pressure, breathing disorders, gastro-intestinal problems, neurological difficulties, infections, and chronic pain, all require medical intervention. Also, medical help should be sought by those who experience threatening weight loss, malnourishment, chronic fatigue, and insomnia because of fasting or other cleansing routines.

Advice should be sought from licensed health practitioners, including but not limited to medical doctors. By adhering to this procedure, you increase the likelihood that services rendered will be within the professional's expertise, and other appropriate referrals will be made when the problem is outside of their area of competence.

4. Serious or Threatening Deterioration of Life-Style Our main concern here is with actions engaged in by individuals which do not support their lives, the lives for whom they bear some responsibility, or the life of the community as a whole. Some examples of the kinds of actions we mean are:

* squandering or giving away money and other assets that deprive an individual or his family of basic necessities;
* withdrawing from society to the extent that the individual is unable to function socially in the most fundamental ways;
* presenting a personal physical appearance, or living circumstances that are not only offensive or repulsive, but also unhealthy or illegal;
* engaging in drug or alcohol abuse;
* abandoning family and family responsibilities;
* physically abusing others or violating their rights;
* physically abusing oneself or presenting a potential threat to one's own physical well-being;
* committing criminal offenses.

In some cases, the group or movement that the individual is associated with might be able to rectify the problem. If they cannot, then referral should be made to the appropriate individual or agency which might include marriage, family, financial, or employment counselors, social workers, welfare agencies, rehabilitation counselors, drug and alcohol centers, or family service centers. In some cases (such as abuse and criminal behavior), it may be necessary or even legally required that you contact police, domestic, or child abuse centers.

We have tried to provide you with a fairly complete, but by no means exhaustive list, of circumstances which would require outside help. Mostly our suggestions have related to seeking that help from health or helping professionals. Whenever it seems appropriate, you may also find it helpful to contact your family or close friends or the family or friend of the individual involved. Obviously, other circumstances could arise where good judgement would need to be exercised. Finally, if in doubt, **the best motto is "safety first."**

Appendix B
Selecting A Growth Program

Finally, a word of advice to those, such as counselors or therapists, in a position to help others. We ourselves have always made it a practice not to interfere with or modify any ongoing consciousness raising program an individual may be participating in. We have a healthy respect for most of the programs which brought these people to us. And we assume that it was the therapeutic and purifying aspects of these programs which allowed these people to unblock mental and physical stress and make rapid gains in the growth of consciousness.

For questions regarding these programs, whether the programs are physical, spiritual, psychological or some combination of these, we refer the person back to the program itself. The best role for a counselor or therapist is not to actively interfere with, or replace, any self-improvement program, but to be a neutral agent in integrating and stabilizing the gains that his or her client has already made. And to those in the position of seeking professional assistance, you can do no better than to find someone who fulfills this role.

Throughout this book, we have made reference to "self-improvement programs" in a rather general manner. We have been so general because it was not our purpose to examine or recommend any particular program or technique, but to offer ways of stabilizing the gains already made through any legitimate program.

However, we do feel obligated here to suggest some criteria by which you may evaluate the merits of a program you are presently considering or in which you have already participated. This also includes the increasing number of individuals who develop their own growth programs for themselves.

PROFOUND: Does the program take into consideration the deepest layer of human existence, referred to in this book as the Self, transcendental or pure consciousness, or the absolute?

COMPLETE: Is the full range of consciousness or existence included, from gross to subtle and beyond? Does the program take into account both the relative and absolute aspects of life (i.e., how to live and how to contact the basis of life)?

PRACTICAL: Along with theoretical understanding, does the program offer practical techniques through which you may gain direct experiences of the Self?

NATURAL: Is there an ease, an effortlessness to both the knowledge and technique, devoid of undue strain and pressure?

REWARDING: Are there recognizable and observable personal benefits in your day-to-day life and the lives of others involved in the program?

LIFE SUPPORTING: Does the program contribute to the well-being of the individual, society, and the environment? Are you sure it does not exploit the individual in any way, such as financially, socially, or physically?

Positive answers to these questions would clearly indicate that a self-improvement program or technique has merit.

INDEX

THE AUTHORS

James Stallone, Ph.D., is currently a licensed psychologist in private practice in counseling and therapy in Dallas, Pennsylvania. He has practiced, taught, researched, and published in the field of psychology for over twenty-five years. His college and university teaching affiliations include the University of Alabama, Slippery Rock State University, Maharishi International University, and the University for Humanistic Studies in San Diego, California. Because of his own interest and involvement over the past three decades in consciousness expansion/human potential movements, he has evolved specific measures for treating individuals undergoing the crisis of growth. It was partly at their request for an in-depth presentation which would facilitate the growth of consciousness that Dr. Stallone conceived this book.

Sy Migdal, Ph.D., is an educational consultant in San Diego, California, with a long-standing interest in the growth of consciousness. He earned his Ph.D. from the University of California, Davis and taught in the California State University system. He has served as Dean of Faculty at Maharishi International University, Vice President of the University for Humanistic Studies, and President of United Training Institute, San Diego.

It is not Dr. Stallone and Dr. Migdal's purpose to endorse or promote any organized consciousness expansion movement. The concepts presented in Growing Sane provide practical self-help for psychological disturbances accompanying the growth of consciousness, regardless of whether you belong to an established program for personal growth or you develop on your own.